Lay It on the Table

A Change Agent in Action: When Tip O'Neill Led the U.S. House of Representatives to End the Vietnam War

By

Linda J. Melconian

Lay it on the Table

A Change Agent in Action: When Tip O'Neill Led the U.S. House of
Representatives to End the Vietnam War
by Linda J. Melconian
Copyright © 2022 Linda J. Melconian
Published by SkillBites LLC
https://skillbites.net/
All rights reserved.

This book is based on the author's recollections from 50 years ago.
It is intended to provide accurate information with regards to the
subject matter covered. However, the Author and the Publisher accept
no responsibility for inaccuracies or omissions, and the Author and
Publisher specifically disclaim any liability, loss, or risk, whether
personal, financial, or otherwise, that is incurred as a consequence,
directly or indirectly, from the use and/or application of any of the
contents of this book.

Paperback ISBN-13: 978-1-952281-47-1
eBook ISBN-13: 978-1-952281-48-8

Dedication

*To my mother, Virginia Elaine (Noble) Melconian,
a talented and gifted writer unrecognized in her day;
and my father, George Melconian, a history
buff who introduced me to politics.*

The motion to table (or, under the more formal terminology of the Rule XVI clause 4, to "lay on the table") is used to adversely dispose of a proposition pending in the House. . . . The language "to lay on the table"—to the extent that it implies that the tabled matter is only temporarily in abeyance—is misleading. The motion is not used simply to put aside a pending matter. The action of the House in adopting the motion to table a proposition is equivalent to a final adverse disposition thereof . . . and does not merely represent a refusal to consider it. . . . In this respect the House practice differs from general parliamentary usage, which permits the use of the motion to temporarily suspend consideration of a matter. Under the modern practice in the House, a tabling action is ordinarily as much a final adverse decision as a negative vote on the passage of a bill. . . .

> —From Chapter 29 of *House Practice: A Guide to the Rules, Precedents and Procedures of the House*

Table of Contents

Acknowledgements

This book is the result of rewriting, editing, and expanding a Master's thesis at The George Washington University, under the direction of the late Professor Ralph Purcell, to whom I am especially indebted for his keen knowledge of politics, personalities, and Capitol Hill. He furnished me with a critical evaluation of many ideas presented in the following pages. I am grateful for his careful reading of the preliminary draft of my thesis, written forty-plus years ago, and for all his thoughtful and excellent suggestions to improve the thesis.

I am deeply grateful to my Suffolk University graduate fellow, Johana Englund, for her willingness and time-consuming ability to use modern technology to digitize a type-written thesis and review and update its sources.

I want to offer a special and heartfelt thanks to Dara Powers Parker, whose patience as my development editor and manuscript coach is unsurpassed and truly commendable. For her reading and formatting my very rough drafts and providing thoughtful and intuitive suggestions to improve this historical narrative, I am grateful.

I want to thank the children of Speaker Tip O'Neill—Rosemary, Tom, and Kip—for their helpful and thorough review of the manuscript, especially Tom and Rosemary O'Neill. I am deeply humbled and thankful to Christopher "Kip" O'Neill for his generous endorsement and insightful corrections.

I am profoundly grateful to Charlie W. Johnson, the former U.S. House parliamentarian, for his detailed and meticulous review of the parliamentary and Democratic Caucus process and procedures discussed in the manuscript and for his astute testimonial.

To Sally Donner, a fellow Mount Holyoke intern in Washington, subsequent staff assistant, and then staff director to Republican Rep. Silvio Conte (Massachusetts) during Tip O'Neill's tenure as Majority Whip, Majority Leader, and Speaker: I greatly appreciate her review and endorsement of the manuscript.

I thank my friend, Tom Birmingham, former President of the Massachusetts State Senate, for his willingness to read the manuscript and pen a testimonial.

I thank Nancy Diehl DiGiovanni for her reflective observations during her read of the manuscript.

Lastly, I want to thank Professor Richard Taylor, my Suffolk University colleague and former Massachusetts Secretary of Transportation, for his interest in the subject and willingness to read and offer critical comments on the manuscript.

Preface

❧

I was a child in 1960 when John Fitzgerald Kennedy, a native son of Massachusetts, was running for president. Kennedy swung through Springfield, Massachusetts, where I grew up, for a rally just before the election. My father took me to hear the candidate speak. Being small, I was able to move in close and shake his hand. Forty-eight hours later, Kennedy was the President-elect. I didn't want to wash that hand. I kept looking at it for a whole week. *My hand touched the President-elect of the United States!* Even though I was only a little kid, that handshake meant something to me.

My first visit to Washington happened a few years later, during the Senate consideration of the Civil Rights Act of 1964. A young teenager, I remember sitting in the Senate gallery with my parents, George and Virginia, and watching one man—Senator Strom Thurmond (South Carolina)—read from the phone book to a near-empty chamber. I thought, *What's this all about? Where are all the rest of the senators? What's going on? What's the phone book got to do with civil rights?*

Then we walked over to the House gallery to watch the action in that chamber. John McCormack was the speaker then, and he was also from Massachusetts. Again, I saw one man reading to a deserted chamber, and I said, "This isn't what I learned about the House in the schoolbooks."

Years later, when working in Washington, I realized what I had witnessed in that 1964 visit to the Capitol: a filibuster in the Senate and special orders in the House. The legislative process was incomprehensible yet captivating to my young, fertile mind, even though it seemed in practice at odds with the seeds of learning about how a bill became law instilled in me in the classroom.

After graduating from Springfield public schools, I was admitted to Mount Holyoke College, a historic liberal arts women's college, where I would earn my degree, cum laude, in history. While I was a student at MHC, my congressman, Edward Patrick "Eddie" Boland, ran for reelection in a tough primary challenge from the mayor of Springfield. That year, Defense Secretary Robert S. McNamara made defense cuts across the country, including closure of our own Springfield Armory, the oldest armory in the United States. General George Washington had commissioned the Springfield Armory in 1777 during the American Revolution. It made the M-14 rifles used by our military in Vietnam combat operations in the early to mid-1960s.[1] My hometown blamed the incumbent congressman for the closure, and the campaign against him was feisty and hard-fought.

During that reelection campaign, I was a proud "Boland Girl." Every Thursday evening, I joined other Boland Girls in front of Springfield's two large department stores, wearing Boland hats and banners across our chests, holding placards as we walked in circles. Some of us would approach shoppers, saying, "Vote for Boland!" It was fun; we were engaging the public and building momentum for Boland's eventual primary victory for the 1968 election.

Those of us who grew up in the 1960s witnessed a tumultuous period in American history: weekly demonstrations against the Vietnam War, frequent marches for women's equality, Black Americans subjected to tear gas and police clubs for claiming their rights as citizens, college students demanding more love and not war. These cultural change movements piqued my interest in government and public service.

The Vietnam War was a front-and-center issue during my college years. It was an unwinnable war, even with our continued military presence, which supported a corrupt regime in the name of democracy in the cold war effort against communism. Even as college students, we knew we had to get out of that war.

By the 1970s, Mount Holyoke College alumnae were well enshrined on the map in Washington, D.C., thanks to our legendary professor of political science, Victoria Schuck. From 1949 to 1977, Dr. Schuck placed college women in Washington political offices, which had previously been reserved only for males. She built a network and cadre of women who had interned, graduated from college, and then worked in professional positions throughout the federal government—in the President's Administration, on Capitol Hill in the House and Senate, in government relations offices, and in think tanks.

Administrative assistants to House and Senate members, as well as committee staff directors who managed Capitol Hill offices, wanted an MHC intern or a staff person who was an alumna. They knew she would be bright, talented, loyal, discreet, and capable; she would possess good oral and written communication skills and the tools to analyze the legislative process of policy development.

While still in college, I worked as a legislative intern in both the Senate (my supervisor, Jane Fenderson,[2] was a Mount Holyoke alumna) and in the House with Congressman Eddie Boland. These internships gave me a solid foundation of how the Senate and House as institutional chambers of the legislative branch functioned procedurally, politically, and in the development of public policy.

After these internships, I knew Washington was where I wanted to work. To be a change agent in the nation's capital was alluring—I could make a difference there, even on a staff level, to break down some of the social barriers that hindered American citizens, especially women and Black Americans. Since I felt I had such a privileged opportunity—given my experience, my exposures as an intern, and my Mount Holyoke education—to make a difference, I sought work on Capitol Hill after graduation from college. I felt obligated to do my part to enable all Americans to access equal opportunity and self-determination.

These were the reasons why I went to Washington. I didn't realize until I started working for Majority Whip Thomas P. "Tip" O'Neill that he shared the same goals and we believed in the same basic philosophy. I accepted the position of legislative assistant in the whip office, where I succeeded Judith Kurland,[3] another Mount Holyoke College alumna, as a professional staff person. I am the legislative assistant who appears at various intervals in this book, which chronicles the House of Representatives during a very charged time in history and its effort to end America's involvement in the Vietnam War.

Politics is the art of the possible. But to accomplish anything in Washington, political leadership must skillfully employ the tools of the trade: compromise, timing, and decisiveness. These skills made Tip O'Neill the quintessential congressional artist. Beyond this, Washington politics is about relationships and how to count votes. O'Neill was the House master at both, educating me first in building relationships and fashioning coalitions of support; he never burned bridges with either members or staff. He also taught me how to count votes; O'Neill would look someone in the eye and directly ask for his or her vote. He knew by body language and verbal response whether that person was with him or not. He could spot a phony instantly!

In writing this story, I wish to share what I learned about policy development at the highest level in our American system of government from my ten-year experience, first as legislative assistant to Majority Whip and Majority Leader O'Neill, and finally as assistant counsel to Speaker O'Neill. The narrative that follows reflects my tenure as a privileged professional staff participant when few women were present or in positions to observe, analyze, or influence the House legislative process. It is based on my master's thesis, submitted in 1976 to the School of Public and International Affairs at the George Washington University. Originally an academic work, it is revised, updated, and expanded to suit a more general audience and to read like a popular historical story, including dramatic scenes that I witnessed fifty years ago and remember to this day. Throughout, I have sometimes relied on my own memory of events, which I have recalled here to the best of my ability.

The result, this historical narrative, is an attempt, in part, to examine the political management of the Democratic majority in the House of Representatives from the key position of majority whip. It is a case study in the legislative process, an analysis of the House's first opportunity to vote directly in the standard legislative process on the critical issue to terminate American military involvement in Indochina. It is not, however, an analysis of the correctness of American policy in Vietnam, nor is it an attempt to shed light on why we sustained military action and escalated our involvement. Furthermore, it is not a verdict on the moral consequences of what happened when we withdrew. Only history can render the final determination of those controversial policy decisions.

Rather, this book examines, at a given point in time, the political and procedural nuances of the daily operations of Capitol Hill. It explores committee action, strategy, and timing. It observes personalities, House rules, and procedures. It is by no means a conclusive study of the O'Neill-Gibbons caucus resolution of 1972. But it does provide an interesting introduction to the legislative process in the House of Representatives. Moreover, it is an account of how the House worked under O'Neill's aegis, while serving as a lesson about how Congress *should* work together for the good of the country (even if it rarely does anymore).

Perhaps the greatest reason I have for writing this book is to honor and commend one man's attempt to accomplish a milestone in the history of the House legislative process. It is a special tribute to Thomas P. O'Neill, the protagonist of this narrative, for whom I was privileged to have worked on staff for ten years— whose political pragmatism I will always highly value, admire, and respect—and to whom I owe all my knowledge of the legislative process, political nuances, partisan coalitions, and procedures of the House of Representatives.

The lessons I learned working for O'Neill in Washington served me well in my later political career in the Massachusetts State Senate, representing greater Springfield for twenty-two years, where I was elected by my senate peers as the first woman majority leader of the Great and General Court. I owe much to this burly, affable, Irish American representative from Cambridge, Massachusetts, and the story that follows

identifies and applauds Tip O'Neill as a legislative ti-
tan, a consummate leader, and a timely change agent
in the House. To me, he was the most genuine human
being I ever knew—a committed liberal and a powerful advocate for working men and women, who really
loved his fellow human beings and whose heart was as
big as he was.

CHAPTER 1

❀

Washington in April Unfurled

Washington in April is breathtaking. The city—dominated by the Hill, where the Capitol, our nation's "citadel of democracy," sits in splendid glory—is never more impressive and ornate. That white marbled monument to freedom shines in a rejuvenated spring. Abundant old maple and oak trees in full majestic bloom shade the wide northwest avenues of Constitution and Pennsylvania, surrounded by the sprawling edifices of America's growing federal bureaucracy.

Boldly blossomed cherry trees proudly line the Jefferson and Lincoln Memorials, the Tidal Basin, and the roads that lead to the Capitol, painting the city pink and romancing its guests. The river, the marble, the sidewalks—each surface reflects and reproduces their color. Every Washington, D.C., school child knows their origin: a cultural exchange in 1912 of friendship from the people of Japan to the people of the United

States. Buses, filled with tourists from all over the United States and the world, park nose to tail around the National Mall. These sightseers come to visit the national archives, monuments, and museums of democracy's revered and picturesque capital.

In the early dawn of Thursday, April 13, 1972, just after the peak of the capital's annual Cherry Blossom Festival, Thomas Philip "Tip" O'Neill, Massachusetts Democrat and majority whip of the U.S. House of Representatives, drove along Rock Creek Parkway toward downtown and his whip office in the Capitol. The cherry trees, in full bloom, waved at him, ushering in a glorious, cool but sunny spring in the peaceful nation's capital.

Yet the House Majority Whip hardly noticed the vibrant cherry blossoms or wondered about any of his Cambridge, Massachusetts, constituents who might be visiting Washington with their families during spring school vacation.

No, this morning, his mind was in the hot jungle of Vietnam, where an escalating drumbeat of American involvement had become a bloody stream of daily updates of body counts. The American death toll continued to climb at an unacceptable rate, domestic protests against the war grew more widespread, and the Pentagon's demands for increased funding of an unpopular war had no realistic end in sight.

As he drove along the parkway, O'Neill remembered that secret plans, later made public, had been exchanged over the past year between the Nixon Administration and the North Vietnamese. He recalled when President Nixon had made public in January an eight-point plan, first offered in secret to North Vietnamese negotiators in Paris on October 11, 1971. Within six months of agreement, it provided for U.S. military withdrawal, exchange of POWs, an Indochina cease-fire, and new elections in South Vietnam.[4]

After the North Vietnamese rejected Nixon's public plan, they made public their own nine-point plan, originally offered in private on June 26, 1971, calling for U.S. departure by the end of 1971, release of POWs, an Indochina cease-fire, and withdrawal of U.S. support for President Thieu's (South Vietnamese) government. Then, on February 25, 1972, the North Vietnamese and the Provisional Revolutionary Government walked out of the Paris talks in protest of U.S. escalation of the air war. A month later, the U.S. announced a suspension of peace talks until North Vietnam desired "serious discussion."[5]

On April 1, North Vietnamese troops moved in force across the demilitarized zone (DMZ), backed by artillery and armor. Shortly thereafter, multi-division offensives were launched across the Cambodian border toward Saigon and across the Laotian border into the Central Highlands. The U.S. responded by vastly stepping up the air war throughout Indochina and commencing naval bombardments off the coast. The air war had intensified during the last two weeks.[6]

As he reached the Southwest Freeway, Tip O'Neill mused the obvious: Nixon was escalating the war all over again. If the Nixon Administration was not willing to bring about an end to U.S. involvement in

Vietnam, then O'Neill, one of the leading war critics in the House, a "dove," believed the Congress should act—and act decisively.

A "dove" was one who opposed American military involvement in Indochina and believed that a congressional initiative to determine the conduct of the war or to bring about a termination of the war was appropriate and imperative. A "hawk," on the other hand, was one who supported U.S. military involvement in Indochina and left such matters of policy to the President.

The Congress was comprised of both hawks and doves. But to O'Neill and the other doves, it was unarguable that Congress possessed the constitutional power to declare war (Article I, Section 8). Thus, it followed that Congress also had the power to terminate the war. It was time for the House, as a coequal chamber of the legislative branch of the U.S. government, to exert its rightful role in the decisions of war and peace.

Indeed, O'Neill had already acted as a House member opposed to the war. On March 25, 1972, he co-sponsored H.R. 14055, the so-called peace bill, or the Prisoners of War Release Act as its key sponsor, Democratic Representative Robert Drinan of Massachusetts, preferred to call it. Essentially, the Drinan bill cut off funds within thirty days of enactment for all American ground and air military operations in and over the whole of Indochina, subject only to the release of all POWs and the accounting of MIAs.[7] By the morning of April 13, the day the Majority Whip drove through a parade of cherry blossoms to his whip office, more than fifty House members, according to Representative Drinan, had co-sponsored the bill.

Identical legislation had been introduced in the Senate by Democratic Senators Maurice Robert "Mike" Gravel (Alaska) and Walter "Fritz" Mondale (Minnesota). Since 1972 was a presidential election year, all major Senate candidates vying for the Democratic Party's presidential nomination to run against Nixon were co-sponsors of the Senate bill: Hubert Humphrey (Minnesota), George McGovern (South Dakota), and Edmund Muskie (Maine). The only exception was Senator Henry Jackson (Washington).

Public opinion polls indicated that the Vietnam War was still a primary issue among the American people. The latest Louis Harris Poll showed that 70 percent of American people wanted to bring U.S. ground, naval, and air forces home and felt it was "morally wrong" for the United States to be fighting in Vietnam.[8] Americans, gathered around television sets to watch the evening news, witnessed the body count rise night after night while their young men waited for their birthdates to be drawn in the draft lottery.

The losses may be compared to the recent experience with the COVID-19 pandemic. During the spring of 2020 and through the end of the year, people anxiously consulted their news channels, newspapers, and online media for the number of COVID cases and—worse—the number of deaths. Americans felt the impact locally and nationally as they tried desperately to stop the spread. And yet the daily death toll mounted, as people all around the globe awaited the day a vaccine would come or the virus would eventually run its course. It was the same sentiment during the nearly decade-long Vietnam War. Continuation of war had become a moral and emotional strain on the American psyche.

O'Neill believed that if the Democratic Party were to be victorious in November's presidential election and gain seats in both the House and Senate, it must take an aggressively active and specific stand for peace in Indochina. He pondered whether the time had come for Congress to use its potent weapon—the constitutional "power of the purse"—to cut off funds for American combat operations in Vietnam.

The day before, April 12, O'Neill had co-signed a "Dear Colleague" letter with other antiwar liberal members of the House, including Democratic representatives William Anderson (Tennessee), Phillip Burton (California), Robert Drinan (Massachusetts), "Sparky" Matsunaga (Hawaii), Henry Reuss (Wisconsin), and Charles Vanik (Ohio). The letter was sent to inform all Democratic members of a caucus devoted entirely to the Vietnam issue, scheduled for the coming Wednesday, April 19.

More importantly, the letter urged fellow Democrats to endorse the following resolution, which would be offered at the caucus by Representative Drinan:

Resolved, that it is the sense of the Democratic Caucus of the House of Representatives that in the 92nd Congress the House of Representatives should work to end the United States military involvement in Indochina, to bring about the withdrawal of all

U.S. forces, to provide for the cessation of bombing, and to effect the release and repatriation of American prisoners of war; and be it

Resolved, further, that the Democratic Caucus of the House hereby urges the appropriate House Committees to take prompt legislative action on H.R. 14055, which is designed to accomplish these objectives, and/or such other legislation as might contribute to the accomplishment of the aforementioned purposes.[9]

O'Neill saw the potential in this resolution. It could be the means to the end of the war. But he also saw the problems, some of which had to do with the substance of the resolution, some of which had to do with the members proposing it, and some of which had to do with potential leadership opposition.

Lay It on the Table

CHAPTER 2

The Hamlet Dilemma: To Lead or Not to Lead?

Following these reflections on Vietnam that Thursday morning, O'Neill parked his car in front of the House wing of the U.S. Capitol and entered the first floor, on his way to the whip office.

The Capitol Building at this time was wide open to members, staff, and visitors. No barbed-wire barricades prohibited outsiders. No national guardsmen surrounded its perimeter. No members or staff needed badges. No security checkpoints existed for members to enter the Speaker's Lobby or the House floor.

As was his routine, O'Neill stepped freely into the open and inviting corridors of the House wing, where he was warmly welcomed by the Capitol police on duty. He graciously returned their hearty greetings. Yet, as he entered his office, his staff sensed that the Majority Whip did not possess his usual relaxed and confident demeanor. On the contrary, he seemed agitated. They guessed he was exceptionally apprehensive about the upcoming Wednesday caucus.

O'Neill's acute political sensitivity told him that the situation did not look optimistic for passage of the Drinan caucus resolution.

He approached his legislative assistant and said, "See what you can learn about the Drinan resolution. What do the members think? I want to know where they stand, if they think it will pass. Get a sense of where we are."[10]

The legislative assistant may have been young, but she was competent and experienced. She had been working in the whip office for nine months following her graduation from college. Before that, she had interned in the Senate and the House. As such, she was knowledgeable about House legislative procedures and floor action. Moreover, she was totally devoted to the Majority Whip. After he spoke to her that morning, she knew exactly what to do. At once, she was on the phone.

During her time in the whip office, the legislative assistant had acquired several sources of information—people working in various capacities on the Hill. During the next few hours, she contacted some of these people who could make inconspicuous inquiries, whereas she, as part of the Majority Whip's staff, could not.

By Tuesday morning of the next week, the day before the caucus, the legislative assistant reported her findings to Tip O'Neill. From a comprehensive yet clandestine survey of her contacts among the staff and among certain Democratic House members, she could make several general observations.

Primarily, the thirty-day provision for a cutoff of funds in the Drinan bill was too short a period for the President to safely withdraw U.S. forces and provide for the return of American POWs. That definitive action of curtailing funds within thirty days went beyond where most members were willing to move. It would tie the President's hands so he could not maneuver a different action plan if the North Vietnamese acted in bad faith. It made the caucus resolution extremely vulnerable, causing problems for some members who would be willing to support a more general provision to give President Nixon more flexibility in the delicate negotiations for the release of American POWs.[11]

Second, and perhaps more challenging, was the problem of personalities. Congress in 1972 was comprised of three types of Democrats: the party regulars, the issue-oriented liberals, and the Southern conservatives. All of these would fall into the category of either hawks or doves.

Party regulars, like the moderates of today, supported a broad middle Democratic position on most issues. Some leaned to the left, some to the right, but they were willing to listen to other points of view and compromise across the aisle with Republicans or with other Democrats to achieve goals that were in the best interests of American citizens. In contrast, issue-oriented liberals put ideology above party consideration and were unwilling to compromise on the issue at hand, even if it meant going down in defeat. The issue-oriented liberals of 1972 were doves—their "issue" being the Vietnam War. Southern conservatives were a different breed altogether in the Democratic Party. Prominent hawks, they voted consistently with Republicans on foreign and domestic issues, and their long-serving committee chairmen carried immeasurable influence and control over the House in its legislative deliberations.

As expected, these different kinds of Democrats didn't always get along. Several party regulars and Southern conservatives were reluctant to offer assistance at a caucus that they believed would be dominated by three of the allegedly most antagonistic, issue-oriented liberal members of the House.

Representative Drinan was a Jesuit priest, derogatorily referred to by conservatives as "the mad monk," and many members refused to support any issue he initiated. Bella Savitsky Abzug (New York), an outspoken liberal, was called "loud-mouthed Bella" on the Hill; Phil Burton (California), coined "crazy-eyed Phil," alienated members with his positive, almost self-righteous attitude about the antiwar cause he crusaded. Burton was also the chairman of the liberal-oriented Democratic Study Group (DSG), a House caucus formed initially by liberal members opposed to the war in Vietnam. All three had already publicly asserted that they would lead the fight for adoption of the Drinan resolution to advance H.R. 14055.

In fact, for this very reason—that the radical and totally uncompromising antiwar liberals would dominate the Wednesday caucus—House Administration Committee Chairman Wayne Hays (Ohio), along with several other committee chairmen, had defiantly scheduled committee meetings during the caucus.[12] These committee chairmen planned to boycott the caucus because they felt that nothing would be accomplished at a Democratic meeting controlled by the ultra-liberals, who, in their view, just liked to hear themselves talk. In their opinion, attending the caucus was a painstaking exercise in futility. Why waste valuable time being spectators to a performance by Drinan, Abzug, and Burton?

From private discussions with several liberal doves, the legislative assistant ascertained that if O'Neill led the fight in the caucus with such well-known and regionally diversified antiwar party regulars as Assistant Whip John Brademas (Indiana), Edward Boland (Massachusetts), Sparky Matsunaga (Hawaii), and John "Jack" Flynt (Georgia) speaking out to prevent Abzug and the other radical liberals from dominating the discussion, then the resolution might have a better chance of success.

Why O'Neill? Because he was probably the most popular and certainly one of the most respected members of the House of Representatives. O'Neill would often share this mantra of leadership with newly elected House members: "The most important thing around here is to be liked by your colleagues." He knew that amiability and camaraderie were among the essential qualities needed to attain positions of powerful and skillful House leadership. As a well-liked and reliable leader, he might receive the benefit of the doubt on a controversial decision or a close vote that could swing either way.

One vote in the House or Senate could mean the life or death of a public policy initiative. One vote could end an issue or establish a new law. One vote could override a presidential veto and alter social, religious, and political values for decades. When a vote was that crucial, O'Neill would look a colleague right in the eye and ask for his or her vote. He usually received their approbation.

Equally important, he was the majority whip. It was the bottom rung of the ladder on the inevitable and coveted climb to the speakership. Thomas Hale Boggs (Louisiana) was majority whip before he became the majority leader; Carl Bert Albert (Oklahoma) was majority leader before he became speaker, as was former Speaker John W. McCormack (Massachusetts). Having O'Neill in the position of majority whip was especially significant to the liberal element of the House Democrats. His appointment marked the first time since John McCormack that a non-Southerner was a member of the leadership ladder. O'Neill was the only higher-up member of the Democratic leadership team who represented the doves' position on Vietnam.[13]

In addition to these problems with unpopular members pushing the Drinan proposal, there was the dubious question of top leadership support. O'Neill had already done everything he thought he possibly could—he co-sponsored the Drinan bill and signed the "Dear Colleague" letter—without antagonizing Speaker Carl Albert and Majority Leader Hale Boggs, who were on the House leadership ladder just a step or two ahead of him. Whenever the issue of Vietnam came up, a small degree of tension surfaced among the three top Democratic members.

Speaker Albert and Majority Leader Boggs, like former Speaker McCormack, were strong supporters of Administration policy in Vietnam. All three believed, as did their predecessors in House leadership, that there must be bipartisan cooperation in issues of war and peace and that the President wielded absolute primacy in the foreign policy decision-making process.

Before accepting the majority whip position, O'Neill candidly and firmly informed Albert and Boggs that he would give unquestioned loyalty to their leadership—a very important axiom in politics and one that he had demanded from his subordinates when he served previously as speaker of the Massachusetts House. Yet, when it came to the issue of Vietnam, it was a matter of personal conviction.

The leader of House doves since 1967, when he had experienced a metamorphosis on Vietnam, O'Neill vigorously and vocally opposed American involvement in the "civil war" on political, legal, moral, and technical grounds. Albert and Boggs, though disagreeing with his opinion, respected and understood his personal conviction. Following his appointment as majority whip, O'Neill tried to maintain a low profile on Vietnam issues at party caucuses and leadership press conferences so as not to create any unnecessary strife with the Speaker and Majority Leader.

Nevertheless, the subtle strain between the two leaders and Tip O'Neill was always conspicuous when the issue of Vietnam came up. Apart from the Vietnam issue, the three leaders—Albert, Boggs, and O'Neill—worked as a team. The Speaker always made the final decision on party positions. Short and introverted, Albert, a Rhodes Scholar, was a brilliant, feisty debater on the floor, a protégé of former Speaker Samuel Rayburn. Boggs, a member of Phi Beta Kappa, was one of the most able men in the House and had no patience with mediocrity.

Since Drinan, Abzug, and Burton lacked the clout and Albert and Boggs lacked the conviction, would O'Neill have to take the lead at the caucus for an anti-war resolution to pass?

The thirty days given in the Drinan resolution, urging "appropriate House Committees to take prompt legislative action on H.R. 14055," was too little time. O'Neill would have to come up with a more general provision to give President Nixon leeway in the sensitive negotiations for the release of American POWs.

At the Tuesday morning press conference, Speaker Albert admitted that he was more perturbed than ever by the Administration's recent actions in Vietnam. Moreover, President Nixon had not given him satisfactory reasons for the increased bombing and American involvement. He was inclined to support a "constructive" congressional alternative to terminate the war.

"Did that not mean you support the Drinan caucus resolution?" asked AP reporter Bill Arbogast.

No, not necessarily. "I have not made up my mind yet," said Albert.[14]

Neither had the majority leader, Hale Boggs.

O'Neill believed that if he talked to both, perhaps he could persuade them to support Drinan's resolution, partly because, in 1971, the dove forces in the House had come closer and closer to victory. A majority of the Democrats, 176, had voted for various measures intended to wind down the war. With the cooperation of the leadership, O'Neill believed the House doves could win in 1972.

Even so, O'Neill faced a real dilemma. His moral convictions came with big risks. Yet he knew how to make crucial decisions in moments of crisis. He understood consensus, compromise, teamwork, and commitments. He had built multiple political bridges of friendships and House relationships. He possessed all the functional skills of an eminent legislative leader. To lead is all about taking risks, and the risk for him to take the lead at the caucus was great.

This was his Prince Hamlet, to-be-or-not-to-be moment. By choosing to act, O'Neill may have been committing career suicide. But the alternative—to keep out of it and thus keep the resolution as it was *and* his status in the House—would surely bring about "the law's delay, the insolence of office" (*Hamlet*, Act I, Scene 3).

He had the opportunity to change the order of things. Should the House continue to support the President, whose actions in Vietnam affected the lives of American servicemen—fighting and dying in an immoral war—their families, and those yet to be drafted? Or should O'Neill lead the charge at the caucus as legislative change agent, asserting the House's rightful role—coequal with the President in the decision to end American involvement in Vietnam? How could he let such an opportunity pass him by?

Would he be able to convince Representative Drinan to step aside and let him lead the charge on Wednesday? How would the members of the DSG respond—would they follow his lead, or would they stick with the Drinan proposal?

How would Speaker Albert and Leader Boggs react to O'Neill leading the caucus fight? Would they support or oppose his efforts? How would his efforts be perceived—positively or with camouflaged doubts by those who, as Machiavelli pointed out five hundred years ago, would not be willing to follow him unless they were certain that he would succeed?

"Ay, there's the rub" (*Hamlet*, Act I, Scene 3).

Indeed, the risk was considerable. The chance of success was marginal. Firmly positioned on the ladder to become speaker one day, he could lose his whip position if he led the caucus fight. He could earn the ire of Speaker Albert and Leader Boggs, who controlled his destiny in the House.

What should he do? He had only one day to figure it out.

CHAPTER 3

❀

The Legislative Process and the Art of the Possible

And it ought to be remembered that there is nothing more difficult to take in hand, more perilous to conduct, or more uncertain in its success, than to take the lead in the introduction of a new order of things, because the innovator has for enemies all those who have done well under the old conditions, and lukewarm defenders in those who may do well under the new. This coolness arises partly from fear of the opponents, who have the laws on their side, and partly from the incredulity of men, who do not readily believe in new things until they have had a long experience of them.

—from *The Prince* by Niccolò Machiavelli

As the Majority Whip was facing his Hamlet-like dilemma, he was certainly thinking ahead. Should he be a change agent on this issue? How does one effect global change, especially in regard to crucial issues such as war and peace?

It was as true in 1972 as it was when Machiavelli wrote, "There is nothing more difficult . . . than to take the lead in the introduction of a new order of things." He continues, pointing out that the innovator will make enemies of those who benefit from the status quo. And those who do not live well under the current conditions will be either afraid of opponents or skeptical of new things until the new becomes the norm.

Despite the uphill battle before him, for O'Neill, this weighed heaviest: More and more people were dying—his own countrymen as well as Vietnamese civilians—and the nation wanted out. Time was of the essence.

As O'Neill would admit, politics is the art of the possible. Any representative who serves in the House is well aware of his or her opportunity to participate in the congressional process by which a bill becomes law. Bills that become laws promise change, "a new order of things." The Majority Whip understood acutely the politics of the House, where an art of negotiation, of give and take among colleagues, transforms one's political sketching (the bill) into the final framed masterpiece (the law).

In 1972, the House system of a standard legislative process had remained virtually unchanged since 1952, the year O'Neill was first elected. Any one of the 435 members of the House could introduce legislation by simply filing a bill, individually or with co-sponsors.

The member places the bill into the "Hopper"—a box on the House floor designated for bill filing.[15] At the end of that legislative day, the Speaker and the Parliamentarian assign a number to the bill, specified as "H.R. [number]," and refer it to the respective committee that has subject matter jurisdiction over the bill's contents. For example, if the bill relates to foreign policy issues, it is referred to the House Foreign Affairs Committee.

In 1972, as when Woodrow Wilson said it, "Congress in its committee rooms is Congress at work."[16] The House committee chairmen were all-powerful, influential, and formidable barons.[17] These commanding chairs of the full authorizing (non-appropriation) committees had total control over every bill referred to their committees. Seniority, unchallenged and systemic, dictated how many years of service on the committee was required before a representative climbed the committee ladder to the chairmanship. Consequently, O'Neill still had three senior Democratic members in front of him before he was eligible to become chairman of the powerful House Rules Committee, on which he served.

At that time, every bill other than appropriations was processed through the Rules Committee. (Appropriation bills spend the money in a single year for programs authorized by the standing, or permanent, legislative committees. They followed a separate route, moving directly to the House floor, generally, with three hours of debate and the possibility of amendments. In 1972, the House acted on thirteen appropriation bills, a lengthy process under the old rules that governed the House before the Congressional Budget and Impoundment Act of 1974 changed the appropriation process.)

Unlike the Senate, the House is not a deliberative body. Thus, bills that come out of the authorizing legislative committees must have a rule from the Rules Committee governing floor consideration. The rule determines the number of hours of debate on the merits of the bill itself, the substance of the bill, and whether amendments can be offered or not, which make it an open or closed rule. In the 1970s, most of the rules were open, allowing amendments to be offered. (Unless it was a tax bill that came out of the Ways and Means Committee, in which an open rule would open up the whole tax code—a highly undesirable circumstance. Thus, for tax measures, the rule might be closed, preventing any amendments from being offered, or a modified open rule limited to certain amendments.[18])

O'Neill was appointed to the Rules Committee by former Speaker McCormack. One of the legislative assistant's responsibilities while O'Neill was majority whip was to prepare him for Rules Committee hearings, which were not open to the public to testify. In these hearings, members only testified about bills coming out of their authorizing committees. After the legislation had gone through the committee process—the hearings, the markups, the drafting, and the redrafting—and been reported out of the committee that had jurisdiction over the bill's subject matter, it was ready for House floor action. Yet the bill still required approval from the Rules Committee to advance in the House.

In essence, the Rules Committee is a premier leadership committee consisting of majority and minority members reflecting the ratios of Democrats to Republicans serving in the House. As such, Speaker Carl Albert viewed the Rules Committee as his traffic cop. Bills that came out of the authorizing committees were always referred to the Rules Committee. Then, the Rules Committee either moved the bill forward to the floor for a vote or held on to it, depending upon whether or not the leadership wanted the bill to proceed. As the Speaker's traffic cop, the Rules Committee could halt a piece of legislation or hold it indefinitely for him so that it never moved to the floor to be debated and voted upon.

However, Tip O'Neill saw the Rules Committee less as a traffic cop and more as a panel that determined how the House members would consider substantive legislation in terms of debate and amendments. The Whip generally preferred open rules, which meant that any amendment germane to the issue could be offered on the House floor.

As majority whip, he retained his position as the fourth-ranking Democratic member of the Rules Committee. Having served on the committee for nearly twenty years, since his second term in the House, O'Neill could have been on his way to becoming chairman of the Rules Committee, which would have been an advantageous position indeed. Yet Richard Bolling (Missouri)—younger than O'Neill but ahead of him in seniority—seemed to stand in his way behind James Delaney (New York) and Chairman William Colmer (Mississippi).

If the committee was where Congress worked, then it was the Chairman who oversaw what work got done and how. Woodrow Wilson also said, "I know not how better to describe our form of government in a single phrase than by calling it a government by the chairmen of the Standing Committees of Congress."[19]

Whichever the legislative committee, the redoubtable "Chairman," in his supreme political wisdom, might assign the bill to a subcommittee or keep it in the full committee for consideration. However, if the Chairman assigns the bill to a subcommittee, then that subcommittee, which covers the specific jurisdiction of the bill, holds public hearings on the measure. During the public hearing phase, the subcommittee receives testimonial input from those among the general public who are interested in promoting the subject matter of the legislation. It also hears from stakeholders who may be adversely affected by the bill.

After the hearing phase, if the subcommittee wants to advance the bill, it conducts a "markup," or a redraft and edit of the original bill based on the public testimony. The markup usually occurs in an executive session, which was closed to the public in 1972.[20]

Following the markup, the subcommittee reports the bill to the full committee. The Chairman may, if desirable, decide to hold more public hearings or an additional markup before reporting the bill out of the committee for consideration by the whole House, by way of the Rules Committee. The Rules Committee then approves a rule, which determines the number of hours that members can debate the bill on the House floor and whether or not amendments can be offered.

House floor action consists of debate for up to one hour on the rule first, which must be adopted before debate begins on the merits of the actual legislation. If the rule allows amendments, they are debated, voted on, and adopted as additions or changes to the bill, or they are voted down and rejected.

If the House adopts the bill, designated "H.R. ____," it then goes to the Senate. A similar process to the House occurs in the Senate. The Senate parliamentarian and majority leader refer the bill to the committee of jurisdiction. The full committee or a specific subcommittee holds public hearings on the bill, advances it through a markup, and reports the bill out of the committee.

The Senate majority leader determines when the bill will be scheduled for votes on the Senate floor. Unlike the House, the Senate does not determine its floor debate through a leadership rules committee. Rather, it has the infamous and somewhat arcane rule known as the filibuster, designed to prolong debate and delay or prevent a vote on a bill, resolution, or amendment.

The Senate tradition as a deliberative body of unlimited debate allowed for the use of the filibuster. Prior to 1917, the Senate rules did not provide for a way to end debate and force a vote on a measure. That year, the Senate adopted another rule to allow a two-thirds majority of the Senate members to end a filibuster, or endless debate, by a procedure known as "cloture."[21] For example, in 1972, the filibuster could end if a required 67, or two-thirds of the 100-member Senate, voted to pass cloture. Then the debate ended, which allowed the chamber to proceed to a vote.

The filibuster has ostensibly been used to protect minority party rights and to prevent the majority party from passing legislation with only majority party votes. It has been modified over the years, and in 2021, it may be subject to elimination or reduced to rare application. Today, reconciliation is another tool that the Senate uses to circumvent the filibuster on budget-related issues. In 1975, the Senate lessened the number of votes required for cloture from two-thirds of senators (67) to "three-fifths of all senators duly chosen and sworn, or 60 of the 100-member Senate."[22]

If the bill, designated "S. _____," is passed by the Senate identical to the House version, it then goes directly to the President, who either signs it into public law or vetoes it. If the President vetoes the bill, a two-thirds vote of those members present and voting is required by both branches—House and Senate—to override the veto. If the Senate-passed bill differs from the House version, a conference between the House and Senate committees managing the bill ensues to settle the differences.

Following the conference, a conference committee report must be approved by both chambers before the bill can be sent to the Oval Office for the President's signature or veto. These are the steps by which a bill becomes a law.

***

But bills are not the only measures voted on in Congress. Resolutions may be brought to the floor, like a prelude or an opening act to the main attraction. And if the resolutions that the House debated in the years leading up to April 1972 told O'Neill anything, it was that the congressional convention of acquiescing and supporting the President's agenda in foreign policy—particularly the war in Indochina—was ready to be upturned.

Lay It on the Table

CHAPTER 4

A New Order—
The House Balks

O'Neill and other members of Congress could offer several different types of resolutions with varying degrees of effectiveness. These resolutions are labeled *simple*, *concurrent*, and *joint*.

For example, action on a simple resolution, designated "H.Res. _____" or "S.Res. _____," expresses the *sense*, or opinion, of either legislative chamber—the House or the Senate—on a particular issue. Its advancement is complete when it is adopted by the chamber in which it was introduced. While these "sense of the chamber" resolutions may have much symbolic, political, and public significance or influence at the time of passage, they have no legal effect.

O'Neill would have remembered a recent foreign policy example of the simple resolution, S.Res. 264, relating to the International Development Association (IDA) Act of 1958. Adopted by the Senate on July 23,

1958, the simple resolution requested the Eisenhower Administration conduct a prompt study of a proposal to establish an IDA as an affiliate of the World Bank. The study examined the feasibility of the IDA, authorizing long-term, low-interest loans to developing countries. Two years later, an IDA was established as a World Bank affiliate. This resolution illustrates successful congressional initiative in the foreign policy arena.[23]

A concurrent resolution, designated "H.Con.Res. _____" or "S.Con.Res. _____," requires an affirmative vote in both chambers and the reconciliation of any textual differences between them. While it expresses the sense of the Congress as a whole, it requires no presidential approval. It does not become a public law, and like the simple resolution, it has no legal effect.

Perhaps an excellent foreign policy illustration of this kind of resolution, which O'Neill would have recalled favorably, was the Berlin Resolution of 1962, or H.Con.Res. 570, concurred by the House and Senate on October 10, 1962. It stated that the sense of the Congress was that

> continued exercise of U.S., British and French rights in Berlin constitutes a fundamental political and moral determination; that the U.S. would regard any violation of those rights, including the rights of ingress and egress, as intolerable; and that the U.S. is determined to prevent any such violation by whatever means may be necessary, including the use of arms; and to fulfill our commitment to the people of Berlin.[24]

Democratic Representative Clement Zablocki (Wisconsin), sponsor of the concurrent resolution, had pointed out to O'Neill that the Congress, representing the American people, had not yet voiced its support of President Kennedy's position, which was to be prepared to defend the rights of the people of Berlin.[25] The resolution was necessary, in Congressman Zablocki's opinion, to show the world that the Congress and the President were united in U.S. policy toward Berlin. It passed the House on October 5, with a vote of 312 to 0, and passed the Senate five days later by voice vote.[26]

While the resolution clearly supported U.S. foreign policy against threatened communist pressure, it was not requested by the Kennedy Administration. It did not "authorize" the President to do anything, and it received only brief congressional consideration.[27] Yet it clearly demonstrated the unanimous congressional point of view that the legislative branch supports the President in the conduct of foreign policy. This was the established precedent set after World War II and one that was significantly adhered to by the Speaker and Majority Leader in 1972.

A joint resolution, designated "H.J.Res. _____" or "S.J.Res. _____," requires not only enactment by both chambers but also a presidential signature. It then becomes public law and is legally binding in nature, just as in the case of a bill.

O'Neill was mindful of two major foreign policy joint resolutions offering support to the presidential administration in power. They illustrate sufficiently the circumstances under which these types of joint resolutions might occur.

The first was the Middle East Resolution of 1957, Public Law 85-7, originated as H.J.Res. 117. It seemed necessary for the Congress to act because the Suez Crisis of 1956 had left, what Secretary of State John Foster Dulles considered, a dangerous power vacuum in the Middle East. The void was complicated by the waning power and influence of Britain and France in that region. President Eisenhower's message to Congress on January 5, 1957, enunciated the so-called Eisenhower Doctrine and urged its support by congressional resolution.[28]

Approved by the Congress on March 9, 1957, H.J.Res. 117 supported the Eisenhower Doctrine by authorizing the President to extend military and economic aid to Middle East nations. It stated that the U.S. "regards as vital to the national interest and world peace the preservation of the independence and integrity of the nations of the Middle East."[29]

Moreover, it declared that if the President determines the necessity of committing American soldiers abroad, the U.S. is prepared to use its armed forces to aid nations requesting assistance against armed aggression from any communist-controlled country. The only condition precedent to this assistance was that it must be consistent with the U.S. Constitution and U.S. treaty obligations. Furthermore, the resolution authorized the use of $200 million of previously appropriated funds, required certain reports, and urged the President to continue to support the U.S. Emergency Force in the Middle East.[30]

Later in 1957, the Eisenhower Doctrine was employed during the threat to Jordan from communist-oriented Syria when the U.S. Sixth Fleet was ordered to the Eastern Mediterranean. It was cited again when President Eisenhower shipped Marines to Lebanon on July 15, 1958.[31] Once again, Congress supported the President by enacting H.J.Res. 117, which became law with the President's signature. This is another example of the historical deference to the President in the matters of foreign policy and in deploying troops to battlefronts abroad.

While O'Neill contemplated the pending caucus resolution, the second joint resolution example of this precedent was likely front and center in his mind, as it had started this whole Vietnam mess. The Vietnam Resolution of 1964, Public Law 88-408, or H.J.Res. 1145, was more widely known as the Gulf of Tonkin Resolution.

Adopted by the Congress on August 10, 1964, it "approves and supports the determination of the President as Commander in Chief, to take all necessary measures to repel any armed attack" on U.S. forces and to "prevent further aggression." It affirmed that the United States is "prepared, as the President determines, to take steps, including the use of armed forces, to assist any member of the protocol state of the South-East Asia Collective Defense Treaty requesting assistance in defense of its freedom." It provided that the resolution "shall expire by presidential determination concerning the peace and security of the area" or by congressional concurrent resolution.[32]

The incidents that spawned the joint resolution occurred on August 2 and 4, 1964, and appeared to be a provocation for war. When North Vietnamese gunboats allegedly fired on U.S. Navy destroyers believed to be in international waters in the Gulf of Tonkin off the Vietnamese coast, the navy reported the incident and subsequent exchange of gunfire.[33] Disputes about what exactly happened persist to this day. President Johnson ordered air strikes in retaliation against the North Vietnamese military. He used the incidents to escalate American involvement in a Vietnamese civil war. Congress complied with his request to pass the Gulf of Tonkin Resolution, which gave the President broad power to conduct air strikes and commit combat troops into Vietnam indefinitely. Though not a congressional declaration of war, it was perceived as tantamount to a declaration. (A congressional declaration requires a joint resolution.[34]) Moreover, it sanctioned congressional approval of presidential action in Vietnam.

In a special message on August 5, President Johnson recommended prompt enactment of a resolution "to give convincing evidence to the aggressive communist nations, and to the world as a whole, that our policy in Southeast Asia will be carried forward—and that the peace and security of the area will be preserved." The President cited the importance of showing hostile nations "that there is no division among us," at a time "when we are entering on three months of political campaigning."[35]

Within two days, the resolution had been adopted, 414 to 0 in the House and 88 to 2 in the Senate.[36] Some members of Congress had argued against giving such a vast grant of power to the President. President Johnson, referring to the air retaliation he ordered, stated on signing the resolution, "As Commander in Chief, the responsibility was mine—and mine alone," and subsequently, "This resolution confirms and reinforces powers of the presidency."[37] (This confirmation of presidential war power would later be challenged by the War Powers Act of 1973. Renewed challenges are resurfacing in 2021.[38])

For O'Neill to chronicle the details of American evolutionary involvement in Indochina following the adoption of the Gulf of Tonkin Resolution of 1964—or to reflect on the growth of war critics at home after 1966—seemed superfluous. He knew the details: some members of the Senate, joined by a few members of the House—including himself—began to question American involvement in Indochina.

The Senate was out front quickly. Under the leadership of its aggressive chairman, J. William Fulbright, the Senate Foreign Relations Committee in early 1968 adopted a resolution that in the future a commitment of armed forces abroad with certain exceptions would require "affirmative action by Congress specifically intended to give rise to such a commitment."[39]

However, the resolution was withheld from Senate floor action because, on March 31, 1968, President

Johnson, in a heralded speech, informed the American people of a cessation in the bombing to obtain a negotiated peace through talks between the U.S. and North Vietnamese in Paris. In the same speech, he then made the startling announcement that "he would not seek nor accept the nomination of his party for the office of president of the United States."[40]

Following his election in 1968 as president of the United States, Richard Nixon began his Vietnamization program to phase out U.S. withdrawal from Vietnam at the rate of 12,500 combat soldiers per month. In addition, he continued the efforts initiated by President Johnson to reach a negotiated settlement in Paris and to obtain the return of American prisoners of war.

In the opinion of O'Neill and other legislators in the Congress, who wanted immediate termination of U.S. military involvement rather than gradual disengagement, the President's Vietnamization program was moving too slowly. More aggressive action, calling for immediate withdrawal of American troops, seemed appropriate.

The first successful attempt to limit U.S. involvement in Indochina occurred in the Senate on December 15, 1969, when the Cooper-Church amendment to the defense appropriations bill passed, 73 to 17. It stated: "In line with the expressed intention of the President of the United States, none of the funds appropriated by this act shall be used to finance the introduction of American ground troops into Laos or Thailand."[41]

Responding to the Cambodian incursion five months later, in May 1970, the Senate passed on May

26, 1970, by a vote of 82 to 11, the Cooper-Church-Mansfield amendment to the Military Sales Act. Briefly, it prohibited the use of any funds after July 1, 1970, for U.S. military operations in or above Cambodia.[42] At the end of that year, in December 1970, the Senate attached to the supplemental foreign aid authorization bill an even stronger Cooper-Church amendment, which explicitly forbade the use of any funds to "finance the introduction of ground troops into Cambodia or to provide U.S. advisors" to or for Cambodian military forces fighting in that country.[43]

As such, by the end of 1970, the Senate had gone on record three times approving funding cutoff amendments to limit American involvement in Indochina. But it had not yet passed an amendment to prohibit the use of funds after a specific date for deployment or maintenance of American forces in Vietnam. That specific amendment, the McGovern-Hatfield amendment, had been defeated in the Senate, 39 to 55, on September 1, 1970.[44]

Meanwhile, the Democratic-controlled House of Representatives continued to support the President's Vietnam policy. Under the careful aegis of Speaker John McCormack and Majority Leader Carl Albert, the top Democratic leadership believed that the President, as Commander in Chief, had the sole responsibility of committing and maintaining U.S. troops overseas in armed conflict. They adhered to former Speaker Sam Rayburn's dictum: "Partisan politics stops at the water's edge."

Following Speaker McCormack's retirement in 1970 at the end of the 91st Congress, his successor, Speaker Carl Albert, and the new majority leader, Hale Boggs, continued to support the President's Vietnam policy. Why? Educated in the traditional school of politics, which taught and advocated bipartisan co-operation in foreign policy, Albert and Boggs firmly believed that the House should be a constructive and supportive partner to the President, who wielded primacy in all matters of the foreign policy decision-making process.[45]

At the dawn of the 92nd Congress in 1971, the Mansfield amendment, with a specific Vietnam withdrawal timetable, was the vehicle the "dovish" senators attached to every military and defense authorization and to every appropriation bill to which it was germane. Declaring it to be "the policy of the United States to terminate at the earliest practical date" all military operations of the United States in Indochina, the Mansfield amendments would "provide for the prompt and orderly withdrawal of all United States military forces no later than nine months after the date of enactment . . . subject to the release of all American prisoners of war held by the government of North Vietnam and all forces allied with such government."[46]

The Mansfield amendment passed the Senate on two different occasions in 1971: 57 to 42 and 57 to 38.[47]

The key yet crucial difference between the Mansfield approach and the Nixon Administration's Vietnamization was the date by which withdrawal of all U.S. troops had to occur. Administration officials argued that the withdrawal date of nine months was precipitous; it would tie the hands of the President, who would need time to negotiate a peace settlement in Paris. Moreover, the Administration argued that setting a date for withdrawal would intrude upon executive responsibility for the conduct of foreign relations. Instead, they advocated a continuation of the phased-out Vietnamization policy.

In the House of Representatives, the second Mansfield amendment, which called for a six-month deadline, was rejected on a procedural question on October 19, 1971. House Minority Whip Les Arends (Illinois) moved to table (or kill) the motion to instruct the House conferees to accept the Mansfield amendment. The motion to table was adopted 216 to 192, thus defeating the motion to instruct the House conferees by twenty-four votes. To date, it was the largest vote in the House in support of an end-the-war amendment.[48]

In addition to the second Senate Mansfield amendment, three other major 1971 Vietnam votes occurred in the House on establishing a deadline for ending U.S. participation in Indochina hostilities, subject only to the release of POWs. Supporters of a deadline steadily increased their numbers from the first vote in April on the Fraser House floor amendment to the draft bill, which, similar to the Senate Cooper-Church amendments, prohibited the deployment of draftees to Indochina after December 31, 1971. That amendment was defeated on a vote of 122 to 260.[49]

Next, the Nedzi-Whalen amendment (identical to the Senate McGovern-Hatfield amendment) to the military procurement bill cutting off funds for the war after December 31, 1971, was defeated on June 17 by a vote of 158 to 254.[50] This amendment is the only one of the three that employed the congressional power of the purse to cut off funds by a date certain.

The first Mansfield amendment, calling for a nine-month deadline, was defeated by a vote on a motion by Democratic Representative Edward Hébert (Louisiana), chairman of the House Armed Services Committee. Hébert moved to table the Whalen motion to instruct the House conferees on the draft bill to accept the Mansfield amendment. The tabling motion carried by a vote of 219 to 176 on June 28, thus killing the Whalen effort to instruct.[51]

The following is a breakdown of these three major votes on the war in the House:

	Fraser Amendment April 1		Nedzi-Whalen Amendment June 17		First Mansfield Amendment (9-month deadline) June 28	
All Members	122 (32%)	260 (68%)	158 (38%)	254 (62%)	176 (44%)	219 (56%)
Democrats	98 (44%)	123 (56%)	135 (56%)	106 (44%)	143 (63%)	83 (37%)
Republicans	24 (15%)	137 (85%)	23 (13%)	148 (87%)	32 (19%)[52]	136 (81%)

Increase in support for a deadline came primarily from shifts among Democrats. Note that in the three-month period from the beginning of April to the end of June, Democrats moved from 56 percent in opposition to a deadline to 63 percent in support of a deadline. Republican opposition to a deadline, however, remained relatively constant.

During House consideration of various Senate-sponsored amendments setting a withdrawal deadline, a total of 223 members voted at one time or another in favor of a date certain. Of this total, 176 were Democrats.

Thus, during the first session of the 92nd Congress, 79 percent of House Democrats went on record in favor of a fixed withdrawal deadline subject only to POW release.[53]

When the House and Senate adopted the conference report to the Military Selective Service Extension Act on September 29, 1971, the original Mansfield amendment had been so watered down in its revisions as it went through the legislative process that it was meaningless. It stated simply that, as "the sense of Congress," there "be prompt and orderly withdrawal" of U.S. forces from Indochina. It was nothing more than a direct endorsement of the President's Vietnamization program of gradual American disengagement.[54]

By the time the House and Senate conferees met on the foreign aid bill, the last item of the first session to which a Mansfield amendment was germane, a multiple number of differences between the two versions of the authorizing bill had to be reconciled. Within three weeks, all the differences were resolved with the single exception of the Mansfield amendment.

Democratic Senator Michael Mansfield (Montana), majority leader of the Senate and ranking member of the Foreign Relations Committee, said there would be no foreign aid authorization bill unless his end-the-war amendment calling for withdrawal of all U.S. troops from Indochina within six months was adopted without change. Thomas "Doc" Morgan (Pennsylvania), Democratic chairman of the House Foreign Affairs Committee, pointing out that the majority of the House members had already voted down the Mansfield amendments during 1971, refused to accept the amendment with a six-month deadline. The foreign aid bill remained deadlocked in conference for the remainder of the first session of the 92nd Congress; it held up both foreign aid appropriations and adjournment for nearly one month.[55]

As O'Neill reflected on the chronology of major congressional attempts through 1971 to terminate American involvement in Indochina, he realized that the question of ending this immoral war settled around two issues: a date certain and funding cutoff. By the end of 1971, President Nixon had increased the monthly withdrawal rate from 12,500 to 14,300 as part of his Vietnamization policy, but he firmly continued to reject any deadline for total disengagement.

While the President was endeavoring to unwind the conflict as rapidly as he felt it was feasible to do, the Congress, in defeating the McGovern-Hatfield amendment in the Senate and its identical version, the Nedzi-Whalen amendment, in the House, gave its vote of approval to the disengagement steps being taken by the executive.

Such was the Vietnam situation in Congress by the beginning of 1972, the starting point of this story. The Senate had passed several amendments to terminate United States' involvement in Indochina by a date certain, the House had not yet passed any such measures to terminate U.S. involvement, and neither chamber had adopted legislation to cut off funds for direct U.S. combat operations in or over Vietnam.

It can be argued that the House never had an opportunity to vote directly in the standard legislative process on this critical issue. The House Foreign Affairs Committee never deliberated and reported out favorably either a resolution or amendment to a bill to terminate the war by a date certain or to cut off funds for the conduct of the war. The Senate Foreign Relations Committee reported out amendments to terminate the war many times. Whenever the House voted on the issue prior to 1972, it was always on a Senate-passed amendment or a House amendment identical or similar to the Senate amendment. It never considered any end-the-war measure on the House floor that had been introduced by a member of the House and processed through the Foreign Affairs Committee.[56]

Perhaps, O'Neill thought, this was the year the House would finally seize the opportunity.

Lay It on the Table

CHAPTER 5

Core Beliefs: People Like to be Asked

Thomas Philip O'Neill Jr. was called "Tip" by his family after an 1880s baseball player who had a proclivity for "tipping" foul balls and whose surname was also O'Neill. Majority Whip O'Neill was the son of an Irish Catholic bricklayer. He often boasted of his Irish heritage: his maternal grandmother's lineage (Fullerton) originated in County Donegal, Ireland; his paternal ancestry (O'Neill) was from County Cork.[57]

With deep roots in Greater Boston, O'Neill grew up in the working-class neighborhood of North Cambridge—once called "Old Dublin"—not the elite, liberal establishment of Harvard's Brattle Street neighborhood. He received a strong parochial school training at Cambridge's St. John's High School and then a fine Jesuit education at Boston College.[58]

Public service was in his blood, and he started early. As a Boston College senior in 1935, he ran for a seat on the Cambridge City Council, losing by only a few votes. It was the one loss he never forgot, which he memorialized in his famous Mrs. O'Brien story. Elizabeth O'Brien was his neighbor when he was growing up. She told him that she'd voted for him for city council, even though he hadn't asked her to.

He was astonished. "I've lived across the street from you for eighteen years. I cut your grass in the summer and shoveled your walk in the winter. I didn't think I had to ask for your vote."

To which Mrs. O'Brien replied, "People like to be asked."[59]

The burly Irish politician from Cambridge won every election since that single misstep by asking his constituents for their votes and retelling the Mrs. O'Brien story repeatedly. Thanks to Mrs. O'Brien, his political career culminated in a fifty-year legacy of triumphant public service.

The next year, 1936, O'Neill graduated from Boston College and was elected to the Massachusetts legislature. It was in those formative years serving in the Massachusetts House that O'Neill rose quickly to the pinnacle of success, utilizing his skills as an effective legislative leader. In 1947, he became Democratic minority leader, and one year later, he became the first Democratic speaker in the history of the Massachusetts State Legislature.

As speaker of the Massachusetts House, O'Neill cultivated his talent for leadership by always exhibiting a positive mental attitude. He exemplified core principles of equality, hard work, and determination, and he developed practical strategies to promote the legislative values he espoused. He quickly learned how to effectively use the Democratic caucus and committee meetings to push through the Democratic legislation. He succeeded in building consensus among the strongly independent Democrats in the state legislature, where, as speaker, he held intact a small House Democratic majority.

A leader in Massachusetts legislative politics, he acquired an uncanny custom of putting elected members in a room and letting them vent, argue, and object, after which they would come together on an issue for the good of the citizens they represented. State House colleagues recalled that he retained this small majority on all major issues during his speakership and never lost a single vote. Massachusetts Speaker O'Neill stood for decency, character, courage, and integrity. Members of his state's "Great and General Court" were proud to serve with him.[60]

O'Neill served as Massachusetts House speaker during the era of McCarthyism, when communist-baiting prevailed in national politics and impacted state and local policies. As state speaker, O'Neill refused to support the McCarthy-inspired efforts to require schoolteachers to take an oath to the U.S. Constitution to prove their loyalty to United States.[61] He saw the mandate as denigrating and offensive to the teaching profession. This earned him unabashed liberal stripes in Massachusetts political circles.

When John F. Kennedy decided to compete for the U.S. Senate in 1952, O'Neill ran for his vacated U.S.

House seat, won it, and was reelected eighteen times, holding the seat for thirty-four years until his retirement in 1986. A protégé of fellow Bostonian John McCormack, O'Neill soon became a member of the influential House Rules Committee under the former Speaker's good graces in 1955. Just as he did in the State House, O'Neill would carve his liberal leadership potential in the U.S. House of Representatives, standing at the forefront of liberal movements for three and a half decades in national public office.

He circulated behind the scenes on Capitol Hill, building upon an unquestioned record of credibility and consensus-building with colleagues. Energetic and affable, he was known as a "man's man," a golfer, and a skilled card player. O'Neill was so competent in dealing with all the House members on both sides of the aisle that he gained a non-regional reputation. As one representative from South Carolina noted, "[O'Neill] knows every one of the members and has no prejudices. He knows no South, no East, no West, no North—he's all American."[62]

Many members have identified Tip O'Neill as the best-liked man in the House. His absolute fairness and approachability earned him the reputation of being "a compassionately human politician who knows the art of effectively communicating with men who are supposed to be, but seldom become, his adversaries."[63]

An outstanding liberal who supported labor, human welfare, and civil rights legislation, O'Neill never latched on to one specialty, as so many Congress members do. In part, this was because of his position on the

Rules Committee, one of the top three prestigious and powerful committees of the House, whose function is to purview all legislation before it reaches the floor.

To members of his staff—both professional and clerical aides alike—O'Neill exhibited the same degree of fairness, openness, and generosity. His office offered opportunities for career advancement and merit. He afforded all his staff maximum accessibility, input, and approachability. No member of his staff was too young or too inexperienced to be tested on writing ability or legislative analysis, making them feel like an important part of the action. He included everyone on his staff in office social activities and treated each one as a special member of his family. Quick to praise, slow to anger, O'Neill commanded supreme loyalty, respect, and diligence from everyone who worked for him.

Among the many benefits of working for O'Neill, one stands out: He was partial to hiring young people. He always had young interns. He encouraged them to get involved and to do their best, and he gave them tremendous responsibility. O'Neill believed in young people, and he didn't discriminate between males and females. He listened to them all. He asked their advice. For those privileged to work in his office, they felt the significance of his faith in them, and they wanted to do the best they could to deserve it. For he understood the importance of good, capable staff as a critical ingredient to successful leadership. It is vital: so many issues require attention, and so little precious time exists to respond to each one of them. Delegation is necessary, and O'Neill trusted his staff to share responsibilities.

***

Whether speaker of the Massachusetts State House or majority whip in the House of Representatives, O'Neill always stayed true to his core beliefs. As much as he was liked and got along with everyone, he didn't balk at opposition. If he felt the cause justified resistance, he would break with the establishment, the Administration, and even his biggest supporters. He was willing to compromise, but never on principle. He was willing to take risks because he would not act in a way that was politically expedient.

This was how he came to oppose the Vietnam War. O'Neill did not come lightly to his dovish position on Vietnam. He listened to his constituents, just as he listened to his staff and other members of Congress.

In 1967, O'Neill was among the first House Democratic leaders to break with President Johnson in opposition to the Vietnam War. Perhaps it was his most excruciating decision in his role representing Cambridge in the U.S. House. Even though the academics in Cambridge favored such a change, O'Neill's strength had always come from the working men and women of Greater Boston, who at that time were still hawkish.

His son, Thomas, reflects that "Dad had to sell the non-academics on his switch. He really saw himself as educating them to the realities of the war. He seriously doubted whether he would be re-elected."[64]

The war issue brought into focus O'Neill's unique situation in representing both an academic and non-academic community. He confronted it, as he explained, by working "hard at representing the people of my district, no matter who they are. If a college needs help, I do what I can. If a person needs help, I help him or her. There is no problem if you look at the job in terms of people needing help."[65]

Cambridge's academic constituents unfailingly supported O'Neill over the years. He was at the head of countless liberal movements, which attracted large numbers of collegians. "Throughout my life," he said, "I have been a liberal. Many times I have taken liberal stands long before they came into prominence."[66]

Such was his stand in 1967, when his constituents asked him questions about Vietnam that he could not answer, even though he had just been briefed by high-ranking Pentagon officials. Privately, some of these officials expressed to him their doubts about the outcome of the war. That was the beginning of his questioning the mission, motives, and purpose of our fighting a war in Southeast Asia. None of the generals in the Pentagon seemed able to clearly articulate the U.S. mission. It had become clouded between fighting communism and imposing democratic nation-building in South Vietnam.

Was there a moral objective as American body counts continued to mount commensurate with more and more combat troops sent to the jungles of Vietnam? For what reasons did the war seem to escalate at every turn? Even with the increased airpower, aid to South Vietnam, and tactical victories, the U.S. and its South Vietnamese allies did not seem to be winning this war—at least not to the point where the U.S. could walk away and the South Vietnamese government and army could hold their own. Yes, the North Vietnamese casualties were great, but there were serious losses on both sides.[67] Furthermore, the servicemen who did return home came with severe physical disabilities and debilitating combat stress (or PTSD).

To O'Neill, this catastrophic outcome was not worth the sacrifice: a blurred mission, an interminable Vietnamization process, a protracted U.S. combat troop withdrawal. There must be a change of policy, he thought. There must be a termination of this unceasing American sacrifice.

Much work lay ahead. O'Neill would have to rely on his own political prowess with the capable staff in his whip office to aid him.

CHAPTER 6

The Whip (Office) in Action

While the whip's position changed over the years, in 1971, when O'Neill became the majority whip, he was appointed, not elected. He was appointed by Majority Leader Hale Boggs with the approval of Speaker Carl Albert.

The succession of House leadership was majority whip (appointed) to majority leader (elected by the majority party caucus) to speaker (also elected by majority party caucus). Both Carl Albert and Hale Boggs had been whips. Thus, the majority whip position was prestigious and very important—O'Neill was the third man in the leadership hierarchy and succession ladder. It was a step forward to majority leader and speaker through the endemic tradition of automatic succession that has evolved in the House.

O'Neill's whip office was very small—four staff, a driver, and the Whip. First was Leo Diehl, the administrative assistant, who served with O'Neill in the Massachusetts legislature and later was the commissioner of the state Department of Revenue. When O'Neill was appointed whip, he insisted that Leo, his best and trusted friend who had managed his congressional campaigns, come to Washington to run the whip office. Of course, Millie O'Neill, Tip's wife, had the strongest voice in that decision! In addition to Leo was the legislative assistant (this author), two other female assistants (Carla McQuaid and Emily Mahony, née DiSimone), the Whip's driver (Ralph Granara), and the Whip. Besides the whip office located in the Capitol, O'Neill had his congressional office located in the Rayburn House Office Building. (Every House member had a congressional office in one of the three House office buildings—Rayburn, Longworth, or Cannon.) The majority party's offices—whip, leader, and speaker—were all located in the Capitol.

O'Neill had been a member of Congress for eighteen years; yet 1971 was the first time he was in a leadership role, so it was a transition. As majority whip, he was more of an advocate than a participant in leadership decisions affecting Democratic members of the House. The Whip's responsibility was to serve the Speaker and the Leader.

His whip office functioned as a service operation in the Capitol, communicating information from the Speaker and Majority Leader to the members on legislation and procedures—any rules changes and votes that the leadership wanted. The whip office was a heads-up to the members on bills ready for markups, soon to be reported out of the legislative committees, then to be sent to the Rules Committee, finally to be debated and voted on the House floor.

Members would ask the Whip directly, or visit the whip office to ask the staff, "Is the bill controversial?" Was there a Democratic leadership position on these bills scheduled for House floor action that members needed to know? For answers to these and other questions, O'Neill's whip office was a welcoming and helpful source to all members who sought information.

The Whip spoke to members constantly, exercising powers of persuasion whenever necessary to support a bill that was mutually beneficial to the Democratic Party and in the national interest. Furthermore, the whip office dispersed knowledge from the Speaker and Majority Leader to the members regarding floor scheduling of legislation, recesses, and holidays determined by the Majority Leader with the approval of the Speaker. Equally important, the communication was a two-way street. Messages flowed from the members, through the whip office, and up to the leadership—the Leader and the Speaker—about the members' concerns.

Every Thursday morning at 9:15, O'Neill hosted an informal coffee meeting in the whip office, also called the "whip coffee." As the majority whip, he would chair the meeting. The Speaker and the Leader would be there, as well as the Chairman of the Democratic caucus and twenty zone whips.

At the time, the country was divided regionally into nineteen zones, with approximately ten to twenty-five House members in each zone. The members of each zone elected a leader, called the "zone whip," who was an integral part of the whip organization. (New York had two whips, making twenty altogether.) These zone whips attended the Thursday morning whip coffees.[68]

There, the zone whips received information from the leadership to be filtered to all Democratic members in their zones. In turn, the zone whips would tell the leadership about problems and issues that particularly concerned their zone members. Discussions covered rules, procedures, upcoming holiday schedules, working Fridays, positions on legislation, status reports of committee activities, campaigning, and anything else of interest to the Democratic membership of the House.

Since the Majority Leader is responsible for scheduling floor legislation, Leader Boggs would come to this Thursday morning meeting with a schedule for the following week. The Speaker would discuss the bills and get input from the whips, asking questions such as: *Are there any issues with these bills? Is there a controversy here? Are these bills for which we should take a whip count? Are we going to have a problem getting the bills passed? Do we want to make sure we have the votes?* The majority party leadership, which controls legislative scheduling on the House floor—whether Democrat or Republican—will not advance any measure to the House floor unless absolutely sure it has the votes.

At the Thursday morning whip coffee, the discussion always centered around the question *Should a whip count be ordered?* One of the Whip's primary responsibilities included counting votes for the Speaker and Majority Leader by taking "whip counts" of how Democratic members would vote on a bill. The Speaker and Majority Leader would decide whether a bill warranted a party position. If so, a whip count of all the Democratic members of the House would be ordered. Here is where the zone whip organization performed its most useful function.

The zone whips would talk about legislation that was coming up on the floor the following week and any other heads-up on legislation that was still in committees. Keep in mind, these zone whips were from all over the country. They were on different committees. They knew what was transpiring in their respective committees, and they gave good reports. The Speaker and Leader listened to the zone whips' perceptives and well-informed comments and ultimately decided, "I think we'd better have a whip count." Then it was the whip office's responsibility to follow up with a whip count.

Majority Whip O'Neill, with the approval of Albert and Boggs, would make up a question, such as "Will the member support such a bill as reported by such a committee?" or "Would the member vote yes on a certain amendment to a bill?" It depended on what the issue was to determine whether the Democrats had the votes or not—whether it was the full bill as reported by the committee, whether it was an amendment, and whether the rule was open or closed. The questions for the whip count were always worded so that a "yes" response indicated support for the leadership position. He would then call each of the zone whips to count their answers.

After the whip count was taken, the leadership would determine from those who answered negatively, were undecided, or gave no report who needed to be contacted directly. In other words, they determined which members were subject to leadership persuasion. Then the leadership would constantly work on these members by phoning them and talking to them on the floor, right up until the hour of the vote.

***

O'Neill or his staff had to be on the House floor when the Speaker or Leader needed him to inform Democratic members of pending legislation. This happened via the "whip call" system to each Democratic office. These are phone messages that include announcements from the Whip of an upcoming vote or other floor proceedings.

For example, whip calls to members would ensue when a member died. The whip office gave that call to members to inform them that someone had passed away, that there would be a memorial service—which members would attend as a delegation and what time they would leave—and all the logistics of how the House would honor that member. Usually, Congress closed when a sitting member or a former member passed away, and the Whip would send out the notice that the House session would close in honor of the deceased member.

Whip calls at the time were transmitted through the Democratic Cloakroom. O'Neill's legislative assistant would speak with the director of the cloakroom and give him the language of the whip call to send out via the phones.

One piece of advice O'Neill gave to his legislative assistant—who, as a professional staff member in the whip office, was one of only a few female staff with standing House floor privileges—was extremely valuable: "Now, when you go on the floor, be careful. Stay out of the Democratic Cloakroom unless you absolutely need to go in there. The boys are not used to having a woman in there, so they won't feel comfortable with you around."

The Democratic Cloakroom was set aside in 1857 as a space for congressmen to store their personal items, like coats and umbrellas.[69] Once an outdated "closet," it eventually turned into an information center and service operation. It had phone booths, and if members were on the floor debating or listening to the issues debated on a bill, their staff could contact them through the phone system. They would call them right off the floor. This way, the members would not have to leave the floor and go back to their office. This was, of course, way before the invention of cell phones, electronic voting, or televised House sessions.

Even presidents such as Gerald Ford used the phone system of the Democratic Cloakroom to reach and persuade Democratic members to vote "nay" on crucial veto overrides. When O'Neill learned about the President's practice, he stopped it immediately, telling the Democratic Cloakroom manager, "No phone calls, including ones from the President, are to be accepted for members during veto override votes per order of Tip O'Neill." One can imagine the feisty exchange that followed between O'Neill and President Ford!

In the back of the cloakroom was a lounge area with a TV, where the male House members smoked and, during late-night sessions, took naps and shared offensive jokes with one another. It did not smell nice and was not inviting to women members of the House.

Whereas this would be considered discrimination today, in the seventies, the House was a bastion of male chauvinism. Merely thirteen women served as representatives in the 92nd Congress.[70] They were grudgingly tolerated by male members because they were duly elected by their constituents and had an equal right to be a member. However, in the Democratic Cloakroom, women were not welcome—whether they were members of Congress or staff—and there were no female pages at the time. Most women members would walk to the House floor, cast their vote, and perhaps sit in the House chamber for a short period. Then they would return to their offices to do their constituent work or return to their committee where hearings were in progress.

O'Neill constantly warned his assistant, "Remember, you are a staff person. A member has a right to be on the floor and in the cloakroom. For you, it's a privilege."

As a young, single woman, the assistant took his counsel seriously, knowing that he was looking out for her. The legislative assistant would frequent the House floor or Democratic Cloakroom when carrying out a whip call or when needing to speak to a member for the Majority Whip. These were some of the means by which she performed her work, and she was careful not to risk losing her privileges.

In April 1972, she used her privileges and available sources of information to inquire of certain members regarding the Drinan resolution and the upcoming caucus in order to report her findings to the Majority Whip the day before the caucus convened.

When she did, her report did not favor well.

Lay It on the Table

CHAPTER 7

"Let Us Be Responsible for Ending the War"

I think the most important thing we have done lately in the attempt to end this war is to try to re-affirm congressional responsibility in the area of foreign policy. There are too many who wish to give the President the entire responsibility for the conduct of foreign policy. Constitutionally he cannot have it, and morally no one man should have it. Just as we are responsible for the conduct of the war, so let us be responsible for ending it.

—Thomas P. O'Neill, June 28, 1971
Majority Whip, U.S. House of
Representatives

O'Neill's keen political instincts told him the Drinan resolution would fail. Armed with the knowledge of three major difficulties impeding success in

the caucus—too specific legislation, clash of personalities, dubious leadership support—O'Neill knew he
had to act and act decisively. To warrant any chance for
passage of an end-the-war resolution, O'Neill would
have to take a forceful lead the next day at the caucus.

It was a move he did not relish. It was subject to
interpretation by his liberal colleagues as usurpation
of Drinan's proposal. Moreover, it was a move filled
with great career risk, as O'Neill feared alienating the
Speaker and Majority Leader.

If O'Neill, as the third man of the leadership, took
a strong stand in the caucus or offered a resolution, it
would put Albert and Boggs in a very difficult position. It would force the two leaders to respond to ha-
rassing inquiries by the liberal press who would try,
albeit unsuccessfully, to coerce them into making a
commitment. Since O'Neill knew that they would be
unwilling to publicly reveal their position before the
vote was taken, the press would then criticize them for
indecision.

In politics, a personal commitment of support is
sacred. A politician's word is his or her bond—it is
golden, not to be given lightly, without deep and pen-
sive concentration of thought, and from which there
can be no change of position (except in extraordinary
change of circumstances) once the commitment is
made. If politicians break promises, their word means
nothing to their colleagues from that day forward.

In addition to demands from the press, Albert and
Boggs were under extreme stress from liberal members to take a position. Representative Robert Drinan

and Democratic Study Group Chairman Phillip Burton had visited Albert and Boggs to request their leadership support at the caucus for Drinan's resolution. The leaders listened but did not respond with a commitment of support. O'Neill knew all too well that Speaker Albert and Majority Leader Boggs would want to leave their options open until the last minute.

Though taking a position at the caucus could further strain the tension between him and the two Democratic leaders, O'Neill felt compelled to act. It was not for political pragmatism alone; but to do otherwise— to sit back and let the Drinan proposal at the caucus go down in flames—went against every moral fiber in his body. It would go against all the reasons he had been opposed to the Vietnam War for nearly five years. He felt it was his duty to lead the caucus as a matter of conscience and as one of the leading doves in the House.

Because he was in the position of majority whip, he possessed the stature and prestige of a leader who lived by his convictions. He would command his Democratic colleagues' attention and support to introduce at the caucus a more general proposal—separate and apart from Drinan's. Yet he must offer one that still had the same goal in mind: a date certain for termination of U.S. hostilities in Indochina, subject only to release of POWs and accounting for MIAs.

The Drinan proposal was not the only resolution on Vietnam to be considered by the caucus. O'Neill's legislative assistant knew of two other proposals that might be offered. One was a resolution the hawkish congressman from upstate New York, Samuel "Sam" Stratton, would offer. The Stratton draft read:

> That it is the sense of the Democratic Caucus of the House of Representatives that in the 92nd Congress the House of Representatives:
>
> Should condemn the current military invasion of South Viet Nam by the forces of North Viet Nam;
>
> Should support the effort to provide adequate protection to the 85,000 American forces still located in South Viet Nam during their continued withdrawal; and
>
> Should urge the North Vietnamese government to withdraw these military invasion forces promptly from South Viet Nam so that meaningful negotiations can be quickly resumed in Paris leading toward a peaceful settlement of the Indochina conflict, prompt release and repatriation of American prisoners of war, and a full accounting for all Americans missing in action.[71]

O'Neill was not worried as he read the Stratton proposal; it was compatible with the Nixon policy. He expected as much and would not be upstaged. A member of the zone whip organization, Stratton was a close collaborator with O'Neill on many pro-labor and liberal domestic issues. Yet on the issue of Vietnam, Stratton was his outspoken and hawkish opponent.[72]

The second resolution had been drafted by the Democratic Study Group, or DSG. It placed the burden for drafting legislation to terminate American involvement in Indochina directly and completely on the House Foreign Affairs Committee and read as follows:

> Resolved, that the recent bombings of North Vietnam represent a dangerous escalation of our role in the Indochina war and a direct contradiction of the Administration's stated policy of "winding down" the war;
>
> Resolved further, that the national interest in obtaining a permanent peace with security would best be served by promptly setting a date to terminate all U.S. military involvement in and over Indochina, subject only to obtaining the release of our prisoners of war and all available information on the missing in action;
>
> Resolved further, that the Democratic Caucus of the House of Representatives hereby directs the Democratic members of the House Foreign Affairs Committee to prepare and report within 30 days legislation designed to accomplish these specific objectives.[73]

Like the Drinan resolution, this one differed from the Administration's Vietnamization process in that it called for a date certain to terminate American military involvement in Indochina. While it directed the Foreign Affairs Committee to take prompt action, it did not, like the Drinan proposal, require that the committee act on a specific piece of legislation. It merely directed them to report within thirty days legislation to accomplish the goal of terminating U.S. military involvement in and over Indochina, subject only to the release of American POWs and information on MIAs. On the other hand, the Drinan resolution did not set a definitive timetable in which the committee had to act.

O'Neill liked the DSG resolution and believed it could garner the support of most if not all of the DSG members, a base of nearly 140 right out of the gate.[74]

Begun fourteen years prior, in 1959, as a loose alliance of about one hundred liberal Democratic members of the House, the DSG was initially formed as a constructive alternative to the dominant Southern conservatives who controlled the House committees and the flow of legislation. But as new and younger Congress members were elected to the House of Representatives, the DSG raised its sights beyond the marshalling of liberal votes and moved boldly into the areas of House rules and procedure reform, the seniority system, campaigning, and antiwar crusades.

However, in the late 1960s and early 1970s, the DSG activists, led by Donald Fraser (Minnesota), John Brademas (Indiana), and Phil Burton (California)—all doves who served as DSG chairmen at one time or another—spearheaded the anti–Vietnam War movement in the House. Additionally, the DSG championed the 1970 Reorganization Act, which made the House record its votes on crucial amendments, and in early 1973, this same team would break the iron grip of the seniority system by defeating three Southern conservative committee chairmen.

By 1972, the staff of the DSG appeared to have an even stronger research arm than that of the leadership. For example, the whip organization discussed legislation in the Thursday morning coffee meetings but did not share detailed reports with all Democratic members. On the other hand, the DSG would publish every week, as a service to its members, a legislative report, providing information on each bill scheduled for House action. The report included a summary of basic provisions; the positions of the Nixon Administration, interest groups, and affected agencies; committee action and views; anticipated amendments; and proposed terms of floor consideration. On major legislation, the DSG provided a detailed fact sheet analysis.

By the end of 1972, more than 140 representatives, including Thomas P. O'Neill, were dues-paying members of the DSG. It was well on its way toward becoming the burgeoning group coalition in the House, and within the next few years, many of its long and hard-fought struggles for reform would become legislative realities.

In addition to the Stratton and DSG resolutions prepared for potential caucus consideration, the legislative assistant had a report on lobbyist activities.

Monday afternoon, the two Common Cause, liberal-oriented lobbyists, Fred Wertheimer and Dave Cohen, had dropped into the whip office. Common Cause, founded by John Gardner in 1970, with a growing membership of two hundred thousand in 1972, was always on Capitol Hill when the issue of Vietnam came up.[75] Since its inception, Common Cause has had a liberal reputation, supporting labor and human welfare legislation. In 1972, Common Cause was particularly focused on Vietnam and campaign reform.

Its influence was mainly concentrated on the members of the DSG, and Common Cause itself was most active in the northeast section of the country. It was well endorsed by the intellectual community in O'Neill's MIT-Harvard constituency. Now that Tip O'Neill was the Democratic whip, he was the only sympathetic member of the top House leadership that Fred and Dave could approach for advice and direction and receive solid information concerning Vietnam.

Both bright lawyers—knowledgeable about the political, partisanship coalitions and procedural nuances of Capitol Hill, particularly in the House of Representatives—they always were good sources of information on an upcoming end-the-war vote in the House. During the week before the caucus, they had focused most of their energy using the phones at the DSG office to make an attendance check on all antiwar Democratic members. So far, so good. Reports indicated that nearly all antiwar DSG members would be present. Both Fred and Dave were optimistic about the outcome. But they cautioned that O'Neill had to play an active role at the caucus if the Drinan or, preferably, a more acceptable antiwar resolution were to be successful.[76]

After talking to Fred and Dave, the legislative assistant recognized that both lobbyists were being too optimistic about the Drinan proposal's chances of success. Like her boss, she knew how powerful the interplay of personalities and likeability was in securing the passage of legislation. A Drinan-Abzug label was all the resolution needed to ensure defeat. In addition, Democratic regulars who opposed the war would see the Drinan resolution as going too far. Southern conservatives would never vote for it, and most importantly, Albert and Boggs were unlikely to support it.

Another group, the POW/MIA Families for Immediate Release—a small but conspicuous organization of relatives of prisoners of war and those missing in action—had endorsed the Gravel-Mondale/Drinan bill. (Recall Senators Gravel and Mondale were the Senate co-sponsors of the same bill that Representative Drinan sponsored in the House). Some members of the Vietnam POW and MIA families and their representatives were on the Hill Monday and Tuesday lobbying for antiwar resolutions in the Wednesday caucus.

Two members of the group dropped by the Majority Whip's office. The legislative assistant told them, "Look, don't waste your time seeing Congressman O'Neill or any other sponsors of the bill. You already know they're with you 100 percent. Your time is better spent if you talk to members who are uncommitted or who oppose the Drinan bill but are open to discussion about it."

As the assistant informed Tip O'Neill of their visit, he recalled that in the April 13th "Dear Colleague" letter he and Drinan had sent out, they had quoted a statement from the POW/MIA Families for Immediate Release:

We families of American prisoners of war and men missing in action believe that the only way we will

ever see our men again is by setting a date for total American military withdrawal from Indochina,
contingent upon release and a complete accounting
of all captured and missing Americans in Southeast Asia. We believe that this goal is clearly met in
legislation now pending in the Congress, in the bill
known as the Gravel/Drinan bill, which is sponsored by both Democrats and Republicans. We endorse this bipartisan effort and urge its immediate
enactment.[77]

A phone call from the State Department late Tuesday afternoon requested the Majority Whip to send out
a whip call to all Democratic members. Its purpose:
Secretary of State William Rogers would appear the
next day at the regular nine o'clock Wednesday morning State Department briefing, open only to members
of Congress. Usually a middle-ranking official from
the State Department briefed the members of the
House at these weekly sessions.

Though the subject of the briefing by Rogers was
not disclosed, it was understood to be on or about Vietnam. How prescient of the Administration to send the
Secretary of State to brief the members one hour before
the caucus as a means of trying to influence the vote
to defeat the antiwar resolution. Yet, to O'Neill and his
staff, it seemed rather late for the Administration to
weigh in. Furthermore, to send Secretary Rogers one
hour before the caucus indicated that the Administration was anxious about the vote. Legislative strategists
in the Administration felt that his presence and what

he had to say were necessary. Rogers's appearance on Capitol Hill was an Administration insurance policy to persuade any possible waverers to stand firm in their support of the Nixon policy of gradual phased-out American involvement by the Vietnamization process.

When the staff in the Majority Whip's office heard that Rogers was coming up for the briefing, they laughed at the ineffectiveness of the Administration's effort. Everyone in the office was feeling confident about the caucus outcome now that O'Neill was willing to lead the fight.

As it happened, foreign policy, especially toward Vietnam, was the primary concern of Dr. Henry Kissinger, the director of the National Security Council, and his staff of more than one hundred in the White House. Perhaps more than in any other Administration, Nixon's foreign policy was initiated, directed, and concentrated in the White House and particularly controlled by one man—Henry Kissinger. In effect, the real Secretary of State was Dr. Kissinger, not Rogers. Always, it was Kissinger who was privy to all the strategy sessions on Vietnam, who traveled to the Paris negotiations as the President's special emissary, who accompanied Nixon on his trips abroad, and who met Mao Tse-tung when Nixon visited China in February. Yet Kissinger never briefed the Hill openly.[78]

In addition to Secretary Rogers's forthcoming briefing on the morning of the caucus, Dick Cook, the chief White House lobbyist, had paid visits Tuesday to Southern conservative Democrats like Joseph "Joe" Waggonner (Louisiana) and Gillespie "Sonny" Montgomery

(Mississippi). Waggonner and Montgomery were leaders of the Southern conservative bloc, who consistently voted with the Republicans on both domestic and foreign issues and who were considered prominent hawks in the House.

In essence, Joe Waggonner was Nixon's man among the Democrats in the House. Extremely ambitious, popular, and conservative, Waggonner was a "plain dealing man" (his home was Plain Dealing, Louisiana). He commanded a large following of support from Southern conservatives, and, as an articulate and able master of parliamentary procedure, he could manipulate House rules to fit the Southern conservative needs. Waggonner operated in the House as a swing voter the same way fellow Louisianan Russell Long operated in the Senate. It was the same for Sonny Montgomery. No matter if he voted with the Republicans, Chairman Montgomery, a delightful Southern gentleman, had the utmost support of his district. He was fond of saying, "I get elected term after term in my district. My constituents think I am anointed from above."[79]

By seeking out Waggonner and Montgomery, Dick Cook was obviously securing votes and doing a check of those among the Democrats on whom the White House usually counted for support in these matters. Cook's appearance was not unusual—he or members of his staff were always on the Hill when the Vietnam issue came up. He was just doing homework for the White House, as Fred and Dave were doing the same for Common Cause.

With all this invaluable information, O'Neill headed for a meeting in the speaker's office. Although in 1971, Olin "Tiger" Teague (Texas), the chairman of the Democratic caucus, had been given exclusive authority by the members to determine and set the agenda of the caucus, he often met with the Speaker, Majority Leader, and Majority Whip the day before to discuss the order of the agenda. This meeting was essential when a major issue like Vietnam was the subject.

Chairman Teague set the agenda to prevent Robert Drinan, Bella Abzug, and Phillip Burton from continually dominating the caucus with Vietnam resolutions. Members of the Democratic caucus wished to discuss other priority issues such as rules changes, organization, and elections, yet they were unable to have a voice when the three anti–Vietnam War liberals controlled the discussion.

Chairman Teague was one of the most conservative members of the House. A combat veteran of World War II, he wore a special lift on his shoe as the result of a war wound. His son was a veteran of the Vietnam War. As chairman of both the Democratic caucus and the House Veterans Affairs Committee, he firmly believed in America's military presence in Indochina. In Teague's mind, the decision to end the war belonged exclusively to the President. Ostensibly, he had no patience with the Vietnam War critics. No way could O'Neill ever hope to muster Teague's support for any congressional movement to terminate the war in Vietnam.

But Teague was a masterful politician: a fair chairman, he would conduct the caucus equitably to

all positions represented—a ground rule for successful politics and policies. For Tiger believed, as did
O'Neill, that the purpose of the Democratic caucus
was to "let the boys openly and vigorously discuss all
the alternative options from which a consensus could
be obtained, and then the Democrats could go to the
floor with a unified position."[80] Thus, it was imperative for Chairman Teague to recognize anyone who
wished to speak at the caucus.

By the end of the meeting, the four members of the
Democratic leadership—Albert, Boggs, O'Neill, and
Teague—were in agreement on the following strategy:
Drinan would be recognized first, followed by Stratton,
who would offer his resolution as a substitute to Drinan's
proposal. Teague indicated at that leadership meeting
that Drinan and Stratton were the only two members
who had requested permission to be recognized at the
caucus for the purpose of offering a resolution.

When Tip O'Neill brought up the problem of
committee chairmen scheduling meetings during the
caucus, the Speaker and Chairman were both livid.
All day long, delegations of DSG members had importuned them, requesting leadership assistance in assuring a quorum for tomorrow's Democratic caucus as
well as leadership support for an antiwar resolution.
The Speaker had already made several calls to the
committee chairmen, who were known to be planning
to boycott the caucus. Teague pointed out that the caucus rules emphatically stated, "Members of the Caucus
shall not schedule meetings or hearings at times when
the Caucus is to be in session."[81]

A serious leadership message seemed expressly in order. Majority Leader Boggs suggested a letter to all committee chairmen from the four members of the leadership. Later that afternoon of April 18, the committee chairmen received a memo signed by the Speaker, Majority Leader, Majority Whip, and Chairman of the caucus, requesting the observance by "you and your subcommittee chairmen" of the caucus rules, which prohibited the scheduling of committee meetings or hearings when the caucus was in session.

In conclusion, the letter declared, "The continuing function of the Democratic Caucus as a policy-making forum is of great importance to the Democratic Party, and we will be grateful for your support and cooperation in this matter to ensure the greatest possible attendance at tomorrow's caucus and at all future ones."[82]

And with that, all leadership preparation was complete for the Democratic caucus the following morning. Yet O'Neill was not quite ready; he still had more homework to do.

Lay It on the Table

CHAPTER 8

❈

A Caucus Convenes

Following the leadership meeting, O'Neill returned to his whip office to peruse the arguments his legislative assistant had prepared for his remarks at the Wednesday caucus. He also had in his hand a copy of the resolution the DSG had drafted.

As a practical politician, O'Neill believed that the real objective at the next day's caucus was to submit the strongest possible resolution that would receive majority Democratic support and give the House an opportunity to have its official voice heard on the Vietnam issue. O'Neill wanted a caucus resolution that would send a directive through the standard legislative process, thus forcing the House Foreign Affairs Committee to meet, deliberate, and report out legislation that would lead to the termination of American involvement in Vietnam by a date certain. It was obvious that the DSG resolution was the best route; the proposal offered by Drinan, unpalatable to so many members, could not be adopted by the caucus.

At this point, O'Neill telephoned Father Drinan to explain the problems with his caucus resolution. Drinan understood; he would still go ahead and offer his resolution tomorrow, but he would support O'Neill's proposal if he saw that his own had no chance for passage.

The "mad monk," as everyone called him, was a Jesuit priest, former dean of Boston College Law School, and a first-term congressman. Drinan had won the election in the Fourth District of Massachusetts by his vehement opposition to the Vietnam War. The only priest in Congress, he was already an anomaly, representing a predominantly Jewish, affluent, and white district in central eastern Massachusetts. A pariah with the Democratic leadership, he sought headlines constantly for his Vietnam and other ultra-liberal positions (he was opposed to the constitutional amendment against abortion and was strongly pro-busing to achieve racial balance in public schools). Drinan was the issue-oriented liberal par excellent. Drinan's "issue" at that moment was the Vietnam War, and he didn't care what the Democratic leadership thought. He often usurped other people's positions—even those he agreed with—antagonizing ideological sympathizers by consistently upstaging them to seek publicity.[83]

But Drinan was no fool. He knew O'Neill was being pragmatic about the situation, and Drinan respected O'Neill's political acumen. O'Neill was offering the resolution to achieve favorable action and to accomplish ultimately the same goal as Drinan—termination of American involvement in Indochina, subject only to the release of POWs and information on MIAs.

Also, Drinan knew that O'Neill's prestige and the respect he commanded from his colleagues would go a long way in helping the antiwar cause. Yes, if O'Neill led the fight, the resolution had a chance for success; if Drinan, Abzug, and the issue-oriented liberals were in the forefront, many members would be turned off. Drinan was astute enough to understand he lacked O'Neill's clout and ability to persuade members to support the resolution.

O'Neill made other calls that evening to a number of colleagues. He believed that if he asked them personally, they would be supportive of his actions at the caucus tomorrow. He called close party regulars who not only had liberal, longstanding records of opposition to the Vietnam War but who were also leaders in their own region. He called his friends in the House— those who served with him on the Rules Committee or who held positions of importance and respect in the whip organization.

His message to them was clear and concise: "I would appreciate your assistance tomorrow in support of my resolution." He was putting the lesson he had learned from Mrs. O'Brien into practice—everyone likes to be asked. By personally asking for their support, O'Neill not only flattered their egos but also expressed his serious commitment to the caucus objective.

All he wanted from those he called was that they seek recognition from Chairman Teague and make a few remarks on why the Democrats in the House needed to give the House of Representatives an opportunity to vote directly on the Vietnam issue. Although not explicitly discussed in any of these telephone conversations, it was understood that a major reason for his call was to ask assistance in keeping the debate from being controlled by the issue-oriented liberals—as all previous caucus debates on Vietnam had been. In other words, he believed the only way to win was if the party regulars dominated the debate at the Wednesday caucus.[84]

As O'Neill finished his last call, all seemed ready for tomorrow. He then informed both Speaker Albert and Majority Leader Boggs of his intention to offer a resolution—a "constructive alternative" to ending the war as Albert had indicated in his press conference. He voiced his desire to earn their support for his resolution, but he did not ask them directly for their vote at that time.

Now, Thomas P. O'Neill had completed his homework, just as the White House, Common Cause, and others had done theirs.

***

At 10:05 a.m., Wednesday, April 19, Chairman Tiger Teague called the caucus to order.

A roll call was taken.

A quorum was present.

O'Neill quickly noted that the committee chairmen who had scheduled committee meetings to boycott the caucus were all present and answered to their names.

While the roll was being called, O'Neill checked with all the speakers he had lined up. He next asked both Speaker Albert and Majority Leader Boggs for their vote. The two leaders vocally gave their support for his resolution; neither would support Drinan's proposal.[85] Why had they chosen now to back O'Neill's resolution? They were willing to change their position for several reasons. They were frustrated with Nixon's re-escalation of the war. Nixon's Vietnamization policy was not working. The time had come for the House to assert its rightful role as a coequal chamber to the Senate on Vietnam. Also, the two leaders were acutely aware of the growing support among Democratic members of O'Neill's caucus resolution. The House was ripe to send a message to the Administration voicing its opposition to the war.

Then O'Neill talked first to Drinan and subsequently to other leading co-sponsors of H.R. 14055. He also noticed that Joe Waggonner was making the rounds to the Southern bloc. O'Neill chuckled. Dick Cook must have promised a public works project for Waggonner's district if he kept the Southern contingent in line.[86] It didn't matter. O'Neill was feeling more and more confident of success.

Following the call of the roll, Drinan was recognized first to offer his resolution. Then the Chairman recognized Stratton to offer his resolution as a substitute to Drinan's. This was when O'Neill rose to offer his resolution as an amendment to the Stratton substitute.

When Tip O'Neill began his remarks, everyone fell silent. Ears strained to hear each word the Majority Whip had to say. He began by commenting on the morning briefing by Secretary Rogers, who told the members of the House that the present escalation of bombing raids was necessary to protect the process of American disengagement at the rate of 14,000 per month and the Vietnamization program. Rogers had said, "If we break their backs now, it will take them two more years to regroup."[87]

In O'Neill's opinion, it was a specious issue designed to involve U.S. armed forces in Vietnam for years to come. O'Neill said that he felt sorry for Rogers that morning. The briefing reminded him of Ambassador to the United Nations Adlai Stevenson after the Bay of Pigs invasion, about which Stevenson had been kept in the dark. The arguments Rogers presented were also similar to those he had heard before from former Secretary of State Dean Rusk and Secretaries of Defense Robert McNamara and Clark Clifford during the Johnson Administration. There was nothing new about the conduct of the war in the Nixon Administration.

In a loud, clear voice, pitched high with emotion, O'Neill continued:

"My long-time opposition to the war is well known to all members of this caucus.

"I have been opposed to the bombing of Hanoi and Haiphong areas because of the calculated risk of starting World War III. I believed that this risk was a factor in President Johnson's decision to stop all bombing of North Vietnam in 1968.

"Many of you in this chamber have supported President Nixon's Vietnamization program because you sincerely believed that his policy was scaling down U.S. involvement in the war.

"Some thought that because the number of U.S. combat troops in Vietnam has been substantially reduced over the past year, the Vietnamization program was de-escalating the whole war in Indochina.

"But events of the past two months clearly point out that both these assumptions are erroneous.

"We are not reducing U.S. involvement in Vietnam. Instead, we are presently in the process of tripling our November 1971 air strength to over 900 attack fighter bombers and over 120 B-52s.

"Now, we are re-escalating the war all over again—"[88]

Chairman Teague loudly banged the gavel. "The time of the gentleman from Massachusetts has expired."

Hale Boggs, himself one of the finest orators in the House, was deeply impressed by O'Neill's presentation. Afterward, he would congratulate O'Neill for his splendid remarks.[89] But now, as Teague cracked the gavel, Boggs jumped up instantly. "Mr. Chairman, I request an additional five minutes for the distinguished Majority Whip."

"Without objection, so ordered," bellowed Chairman Teague. O'Neill continued:

"A vote for my resolution is a vote by the caucus to direct, for the first time, the House Foreign

Affairs Committee to consider and act on legislation to end U.S. military involvement in and over Indochina and to obtain the release of American POWs and information on those missing in action.

"This resolution forces the committee to act. It directs the committee to work out, in its best judgment, legislation that will end our involvement in Vietnam. The committee will draft its own proposal. This is their legislative prerogative." He was certainly not trying to usurp the committee's responsibility.

"But it is our duty as legislators, it is our duty as Democrats, to establish a party position and to come forth with the best possible proposal to end the war."[90]

When O'Neill finished speaking, a burst of applause broke out.

CHAPTER 9

❀

Surprise, Surprise!
Parliamentary Maneuvering

"**D**oes anyone else seek recognition?" quipped the Chairman.

Edmond Augustus "Ed" Edmondson (Oklahoma) quietly rose. In a move that surprised O'Neill, Chairman Teague, Father Drinan, and most everyone else, he offered the following amendment to the Drinan resolution:

> Resolved, that it is the sense of the Democratic Caucus of the House of Representatives that in the 92nd Congress the House of Representatives should work to end the United States military involvement in Indochina, to bring about the withdrawal of all U.S. forces, to provide for the cessation of bombing, and to effect the release and repatriation of American prisoners of war; and be it

Resolved, further, that the Democratic Caucus of the House hereby urges the appropriate House Committee(s) to take prompt legislative action.[91]

After Edmondson offered his amendment, the floor was open for discussion on the four proposals. Debate would be cut off at 11:20 a.m., since the House went into session at noon, preceded by a Speaker's press conference at 11:50. These time constraints allowed for only one thirty-minute roll call vote. House parliamentary procedure dictated that it would be a vote on the amendment to the Drinan resolution—Edmondson's proposal.

"You've messed everything up real nicely," O'Neill snapped at Edmondson.[92]

His proposal really was a surprise, and there appeared to be no preplanning involved. Edmondson would have known about the language of O'Neill's amendment from the Whip's staff. In fact, during the caucus, while Drinan and Stratton were offering their resolutions, Edmondson took Drinan's proposal and started rewriting the last paragraph to make it more general and thus, he believed, of wider appeal.

O'Neill would not support the Edmondson amendment. Its passage endangered his more emphatic proposal since it put no time limit on any House committee to act, especially the Foreign Affairs Committee, which had jurisdiction over foreign policy issues. Moreover, it had absolutely no binding effect on the Democratic members of the Foreign Affairs Committee. They could, in effect, simply ignore and forget about it. O'Neill knew this was a key and deliberate omission by Edmondson. And this crucial difference between his and Edmondson's proposals was illuminated by the party regulars O'Neill had solicited to participate in the debate.[93]

The clock struck 11:20.

"All time has expired. The vote is on the amendment offered by the gentleman from Oklahoma, Mr. Edmondson," Chairman Teague announced.

The vote on the Edmondson amendment to the Drinan resolution was taken immediately. The result: 105 yeas, 97 nays.[94] By a narrow margin, the caucus adopted the Edmondson amendment to the Drinan resolution.

Then the caucus was promptly adjourned until ten o'clock Thursday morning.

What did all this parliamentary maneuvering at the caucus demonstrate? First, it showed that House Democrats had flatly and unequivocally rejected the Drinan resolution. They refused to put themselves on record in favor of specific legislation, which, through a cutoff of funds, could terminate all American military activities throughout Indochina within thirty days.

O'Neill, a master of House procedure gleaned from his sixteen years' service on the Rules Committee, knew how to exploit a parliamentary situation to his advantage. The most favorable position for his resolution would be to offer it at the right time in order to get the first vote. Having used this strategy many times in Rules Committee deliberations, O'Neill recognized that in a close vote between alternative proposals, his resolution had a greater chance of success if it were voted on first. Edmondson had thwarted O'Neill's strategical advantage by assuring a vote first on his proposed amendment.

Yet all hope was not lost. Edmondson may have inadvertently done O'Neill a favor. O'Neill had carefully laid the groundwork for the consideration of his substitute resolution the following morning. With the first vote on the Edmondson amendment out of the way, the Democrats could now focus directly on O'Neill's proposal. He could only guess at this point how the vote would go.

***

Following the adjournment of the caucus, Drinan held an extemporaneous press conference in the Speaker's Lobby, adjacent to the House floor. He informed reporters that he had switched to the somewhat "milder substitute" sponsored by the Whip. He expressed optimism about its passage at Thursday's caucus.

"The hopes of all peace legislators are pinned on this opportunity to enable the House to vote directly on the Vietnam issue." Drinan further predicted that the resolution would be adopted by the caucus, "since 176 Democrats had voted at one time or another to set a deadline on ending the war."[95]

This may have been correct, but Edmondson had truly shocked O'Neill. Had *his* resolution been voted on that Wednesday morning, O'Neill was confident of its passage. Now, with the vote postponed twenty-four hours, he was not so sure—anything could happen. All kinds of pressure could be exerted to change positions.

What had enticed Edmondson, a zone whip and co-chairman of the Democratic Congressional Campaign Dinner with O'Neill, to offer a resolution that would not only upstage his good friend Tip but possibly ruin the chances for passage of the O'Neill version?[96]

It should be remembered that 1972 was an election year. Edmondson was giving up a safe House seat in the second district of Oklahoma to run for the Senate seat vacated by Fred Harris. He had an uphill battle. If he offered a compromise caucus resolution on the war that would unite the various moderate to conservative factions in the House, the Speaker might be grateful. Albert, a fellow Oklahoman, was campaigning for Edmondson for the open Senate seat. As Speaker, Albert enjoyed overwhelming support and admiration from Oklahomans throughout the state. Edmondson could gain much political mileage back home by pleasing Albert.

Equally important, his type of watered-down resolution might earn strong support from the Speaker and Majority Leader because it gave them favor with both the liberals and the committee chairmen. The two leaders could say to the liberals that they had gone on record in support of an end-the-war resolution; to the committee chairmen, they could say they had voted for this ineffective, compromised version merely to pacify the liberals. Albert and Boggs had been subjected all week long to an unbelievable amount of pressure from

committee chairmen on one side and liberals supporting an end-the-war resolution on the other side. Any
effective compromise, palatable to both sides, would
be welcomed.

Within minutes after the caucus adjourned, O'Neill
began to prepare for the following day. He went first to
see the Speaker and Majority Leader, to point out once
again how imperative it was for a quorum to be present
at the caucus tomorrow. Albert and Boggs agreed.

The leadership sent another notice to the committee chairmen "reiterating the request contained in
our letter of April 18 and asking that your committee
not schedule any meetings tomorrow in accordance
with the provisions of Rule 3 of the Democratic Caucus Rules." In a conciliatory vein, the letter ended,
"We recognize that this may cause your committee
great inconvenience and are deeply grateful for your
cooperation."[97]

O'Neill then asked the Speaker and Majority
Leader if their tacit commitment in support of his
resolution still held for Thursday's caucus vote. Both
leaders assured him confidentially of their continued
support.[98]

Next, it was necessary for O'Neill to ensure that all
of his supporters were present at the caucus. He called
the same party regulars he had engaged to speak on
behalf of his resolution at Wednesday's caucus. They
would be present and ready to help on Thursday as
well.

O'Neill's legislative assistant contacted Fred and
Dave of Common Cause, who indicated that they would

do an attendance check on all the DSG members opposed to the war. With Fred and Dave's help, O'Neill drafted and sent a letter to each Democratic colleague, informing them of the importance of a favorable vote on his resolution and requesting a good attendance at the caucus in the morning. The letter read:

> The United States has played a major role in the tragic Indochina war for more than a decade. We have given the lives of our precious youth, our supplies and financial resources, and our country has been divided over this war. More than three years have passed since President Richard Nixon was elected on a pledge to end the Indochina war.
>
> Recent events have demonstrated once again that Congressional action is essential to end U.S. military involvement in Indochina and obtain the return of our prisoners. Everyone wants this tragic war brought to an end.[99]

According to parliamentary procedure, the first order of business at the Thursday caucus was an up or down vote on the O'Neill resolution. But the legislative assistant learned Wednesday afternoon from Common Cause that the O'Neill language would be challenged by Sam Melville Gibbons (Florida) on behalf of several caucus members, mostly Southern Democrats who preferred simply to condemn North Vietnam's attack on South Vietnam across the DMZ.

In other words, Gibbons, an ambitious Florida congressman and leader of a small group of newer and liberal Southern members of the DSG, wanted to offer an amendment to O'Neill's resolution, which would include language from Stratton's substitute:

> That it is the sense of the Democratic Caucus of the House of Representatives that in the 92nd Congress, the House of Representatives:
>
>   Should condemn the current military invasion of South Vietnam by the forces of North Vietnam.[100]

The remainder of the amendment was identical to O'Neill's version.

The challenge presented by Gibbons was clearly parliamentary in nature. Gibbons wanted a procedural ruling from the Chairman to offer his amendment at the beginning of the caucus. Because he would be amending O'Neill's resolution, parliamentary procedure called for a vote first on the Gibbons proposal, which most likely would be adopted. If this maneuver were allowed and the Gibbons amendment adopted, O'Neill's resolution would never get a vote.

When his assistant informed him of the threat posed by Gibbons's proposal, O'Neill responded immediately by contacting Chairman Teague. As O'Neill understood the parliamentary situation, an agreement had been reached at the Wednesday caucus that no debate or amendments to the O'Neill, Stratton, or Drinan proposals would be allowed after 11:20 that day. Then, shortly after 11:20, on a parliamentary inquiry by Joe Waggonner, Teague had reaffirmed his ruling that votes on all pending amendments must proceed without any further debate or introduction of additional amendments.

"Is my interpretation correct?" O'Neill asked him. Teague confirmed.[101]

Even with this direct confirmation, O'Neill was ready for anything. In the event that the Chairman attempted to reverse his Wednesday position by permitting the introduction of Gibbons's amendment, O'Neill would challenge this action by calling for a caucus vote on the reversal of the agreement.[102]

Once again, by looking into the parliamentary situation, by directly asking for the support of the Speaker and Majority Leader, and by sending out another "Dear Colleague" letter, O'Neill made sure that all bases were covered for the Thursday caucus. He had diligently completed his homework.

***

On Thursday morning, the caucus was called to order at ten o'clock. As Sam Gibbons quickly rose to offer an amendment, Chairman Teague ruled him out of order and called immediately for the ayes and nays on the O'Neill amendment to the Stratton substitute.

It was overwhelmingly adopted 135 to 66, with one voting present.[103] Next, Gibbons offered his proposal as a perfecting amendment to the O'Neill resolution, which was in order. It was adopted 186 to 16, with one voting present.

The final version of the O'Neill-Gibbons resolution read as follows:

That it is the sense of the Democratic Caucus of the House of Representatives that in the 92nd Congress, the House of Representatives:

Should condemn the current military invasion of South Vietnam by the forces of North Vietnam.

Resolved, that the recent bombings of North Vietnam represent a dangerous escalation of our role in the Indochina war and a direct contradiction of the Administration's stated policy of "winding down" the war;

Resolved further, that the national interest in obtaining a permanent peace with security would best be served by promptly setting a date to terminate all U.S. military involvement in and over Indochina, subject only to obtaining the release of our prisoners of war and all available information on the missing in action;

Resolved further, that the Democratic Caucus of the House of Representatives hereby directs the Democratic members of the House Foreign Affairs Committee to prepare and report within 30 days legislation designed to accomplish these specific objectives.[104]

Final passage vote on the O'Neill-Gibbons caucus resolution was 144 to 58.[105]

Immediately following the adjournment of the caucus, Father Drinan exclaimed, as a reporter grabbed him leaving the House chamber, "The hawks couldn't believe it was happening. It's a major revolution."[106]

O'Neill was pleased by the results. "I didn't think the vote would be that strong," he said. "It was more than two to one in favor of the resolution. Adoption sets in motion the process by which the House can now have a direct vote on the termination of American involvement in Vietnam, subject to the POW and MIA conditions."

He continued, "This was the purpose of my resolution. I believe that the House must reassert its rightful role in the determination of American foreign policy. And the truth of the matter is, the House has a right to set a date for the termination of American involvement in Indochina."[107]

Thomas Morgan (Pennsylvania), chairman of the House Foreign Affairs Committee, at which the resolution was directed, pledged that he would hold hearings "forthwith" on the legislation. When asked if he felt bound by the caucus vote, considering his long-held opposition to end-the-war legislation, Morgan said, "I am first a Democrat."[108]

***

What was the impact of this unusual caucus action? It connoted several significant steps taken by the Democratic caucus: (1) condemnation of the Nixon Administration for its "dangerous escalation" of the war, (2) condemnation of North Vietnam for its invasion of South Vietnam, and (3) unusual instructions to the House Foreign Affairs Committee to act.

Indeed, the House Democrats had handed the White House strategists a definite setback. Until this point, the Administration could always rely upon a coalition of conservative and moderate Democrats and Republicans in the House to block a direct vote on end-the-war amendments approved by the Senate. This reliance no longer held.

The caucus action demonstrated a decisive shift in sentiment among Democrats in favor of end-the-war legislation. That put 71 percent of Democrats in support of the deadline, com pared with the previous high of 63 percent.[109] Adoption of the O'Neill-Gibbons resolution was regarded by the antiwar bloc as a major breakthrough in their efforts to obtain full House approval of legislation to terminate the war in Indochina. Now, the chances for favorable consideration of end-the-war legislation in the Foreign Affairs Committee seemed assured.

Why had the O'Neill-Gibbons resolution passed? Several reasons seem obvious. Tip O'Neill's affable personality and political reasonableness were instrumental to its success. His decision to take a commanding lead at the caucus, despite the potential risks, for adoption of an end-the-war resolution removed Drinan and the other issue-oriented liberals from the forefront. Thus, his leadership prevented the usual personality alienation on the Vietnam issue. And substantively, O'Neill's general provision was more palatable. It had a wider appeal to the whole spectrum of the Democratic membership in the House than the very specific mandate offered by Drinan.

Additionally, the timing of the vote was crucial. It was an election year, and the Democrats, especially Speaker Albert and Majority Leader Boggs, were dissatisfied with Nixon's management of the war. The break-up of the negotiations between the United States and North Vietnam in Paris earlier in 1972 and the expansion of the air war in March and early April, despite continued Vietnamization, provided the political and change opportunity for the passage of an end-the-war resolution.

Only O'Neill in his well-respected position as the House majority whip could muster support from Albert and Boggs. Perhaps his greatest contribution to the success of the resolution was his willingness and courage to take a stand on his political conviction and to risk alienating himself from the leadership. He realized that the chance for a successful end-the-war caucus resolution in 1972 was the greatest since the Vietnam issue had first troubled the American populace a decade ago. Although O'Neill was careful to inform the two top House Democratic leaders of his intentions, and though he constantly consulted Drinan, he had to tread carefully so as not to alienate anyone or to look as if he were trying to usurp the stage from other members.

Yet his political instincts dictated that he had to steer the debate from the issue-oriented liberals to maximize any chance for success. O'Neill had done his homework thoroughly, ascertaining the parliamentary situation and lining up members to speak on behalf of his proposal. He consulted supporters in the days before the caucus vote, sent out a "Dear Colleague" letter, and worked with lobbyists like Common Cause, who were useful in promulgating to liberal members the significance of being present at the caucus and supporting O'Neill's resolution.

O'Neill's mastery of parliamentary procedure and political maneuvering sustained his successful efforts throughout the course of the caucus consideration of this issue. The timing was ripe; the opportunity was there. O'Neill seized the moment. He exercised remarkable leadership, relying on his own well-honed political acumen, not waiting for others to act. He was the kind of change agent Machiavelli would have prescribed and admired. Still, he had to assess the situation correctly if any end-the-war resolution was to be successful. O'Neill—the most popular member of the House, a masterful parliamentarian in his own right, and a pragmatic politician par excellence—was the right person to lead the caucus in support of an end-the-war resolution.

With the passage of the O'Neill-Gibbons caucus resolution, the scene of activity now shifted from the Majority Whip to the House Committee on Foreign Affairs.

CHAPTER 10

Will the House Committee Accept Its Independent Role in Foreign Policy?

The long dormant House Foreign Affairs Committee, which has tended to be an acquiescent partner to the Executive branch, is staking out a more active, independent role in the formulation of foreign policy. It now appears that the House Committee will join the Senate Foreign Relations Committee in insisting upon a critical, advisory role in foreign policy.

—John Finney, *The New York Times*, 1971

The implementation of the O'Neill caucus resolution was an unequivocal directive to the Democratic members of the House Foreign Affairs Committee to report some form of end-the-war legislation to the full House within thirty days.

Several questions could be posed before the House Foreign Affairs Committee began its deliberation on this unprecedented charge:

1. What were the chances the committee would report out legislation that would favorably carry out the intent of the O'Neill caucus resolution?
2. How did the House Foreign Affairs Committee compare to its counterpart in the Senate, the Committee on Foreign Relations?
3. What was its chairman like?
4. What was the ideological makeup of the Democrats on the committee?
5. How did the members of the committee view their role in foreign policy determination?

Before we can address the first question, we must answer the others, one by one, beginning with the second: how the House Committee compares to its Senate counterpart. And to do that, a little background on both committees is essential.

Established in 1822 as a standing committee[110] in the House, the Foreign Affairs Committee did not have much involvement in foreign policy prior to World War II. While somewhat similar in name, it did not share all the constitutional powers of the Senate's Foreign Relations Committee during the first 150 years of America's burgeoning status as a democratic republic.[111]

In contrast, the Committee on Foreign Relations, established in 1816, was one of the original ten standing committees of the Senate. It was perceived by many members in the late 1960s and 1970s as all-powerful. It derived its prestigious status as one of the three leading committees in the Senate, along with the Finance Committee and the Judiciary Committee.[112]

The U.S. Constitution grants the Senate sole responsibility to give "advice and consent" to American ambassadors, nominated by presidents and serving abroad, and to treaties negotiated by presidents with foreign countries.[113] Thus, the Senate plays a major role in American foreign policy and carries out that role through its Foreign Relations Committee, which has jurisdiction in all matters of war and peace and international relations.

It is important to note that the Senate Committee at times supports and at other times opposes presidential foreign initiatives. For example, the Foreign Relations Committee was instrumental in rejecting the Versailles Treaty and throughout its history has questioned Administration foreign policies.[114]

Both the Senate and House Committees, then and today, exercise oversight and jurisdiction over bills affecting foreign policy programs and investigate congressional concerns of U.S. foreign policy. Specifically, both committees are responsible for overseeing the funding of foreign aid programs and arms sales and so contribute to the shaping of U.S. foreign policy. Despite these shared responsibilities, the House committee in the early 1970s did not receive the Senate's acclaim in such matters.

Perhaps the most important power the Constitution grants to the Congress (both branches) in matters of foreign policy is the power to declare war. A declaration of war originates in both the House Foreign Affairs and Senate Foreign Relations Committees. It is a joint resolution, which requires both the House and Senate to adopt, and is signed into law by the President.

Recall, however, House joint resolution (H.J.Res.) 1145, the Gulf of Tonkin Resolution. Enacted in 1964, it stated: "Congress approves and supports the determination of the President, as Commander in Chief, to take all necessary measures to repeal any armed attack against the forces of the United States and to prevent any further aggression." Congress took this action to ratify the war in Vietnam, but it was never considered a formal congressional declaration of war. Rather, it served as a substitute for a war declaration and would provide a congressional incentive nearly ten years later to enact the War Powers Act in 1973. In any case, the Committees on Foreign Relations and Foreign Affairs are responsible for reporting out legislation, which could result in a declaration of war.

In the early 1970s, the House Committee on Foreign Affairs lacked the prestige of the three leading House committees: Rules, Ways and Means, and Appropriations. Politically, there was nothing to gain from being a member of the Foreign Affairs Committee; it was an unpopular and insignificant committee, often the last choice assignment for freshmen members of the House. It was not the place for any ambitious member to attain recognition, prestige, or acclaim in a legislative body overly concerned with domestic pocketbook issues.

However, following World War II, a new role emerged for the Foreign Affairs Committee. It suddenly shared equal legislative responsibility and approval with its Senate counterpart in authorizing the Arms Control Agency; the Marshall Plan; the Truman Doctrine; foreign aid legislation; special economic and military assistance to NATO, SEATO, and CENTO; the Peace Corps; and Radio Free Europe.[115]

Yet even with this equal legislative authorizing responsibility, it still took a back seat to the Senate Foreign Relations Committee. The standard joke among staffers on Capitol Hill in the post-WWII era was that the Senate Committee had relations (implying long-term commitments) while the House Committee had merely affairs (suggesting short-term encounters).

At the time of the O'Neill caucus resolution, congressional committees tended to assume the character and behavior of their chairmen. This can be seen in vivid contrast when comparing the Senate Committee's Chairman, J. William Fulbright, and his pugnacious stance on Vietnam with Chairman Thomas Morgan of the House Committee and his don't-rock-the-boat approach to foreign policy. And so, to answer the third question prompted by the caucus resolution directive, we must take a close look at the House Committee Chairman as measured against the Senate Committee Chairman.

Senator Fulbright (Arkansas), the publicity-seeking prima donna who chaired the Senate Foreign Relations Committee, had strong convictions about congressional prerogatives in foreign policy, and he was extremely successful in generating debate on such issues. He insisted that Congress should reassert a measure of authority, and he believed that a marked constitutional imbalance existed between the executive and legislative branches of government over foreign policy. Under Fulbright, the Senate Foreign Relations Committee was much more assertive and aggressive than its House counterpart. During the 1960s, Chairman Fulbright and his committee challenged both the Johnson and Nixon Administrations' involvement in Southeast Asia.

Yet the House Committee, under the cautious aegis of Chairman Thomas Morgan, viewed its function as a "constructive evaluator and subordinate partner in a permanent alliance with the executive."[116] It consistently gave strong bipartisan support to foreign policy decisions initiated by the Johnson and Nixon Administrations because Chairman Morgan believed that "the President is solely responsible for foreign policy, and it needs to be on a bipartisan basis."[117]

Like many of his contemporaries—including Speaker Albert, Majority Leader Boggs, and their predecessors, Speaker Rayburn and Speaker McCormack—Chairman Morgan was brought up in the postwar Congressional School of Philosophy, which instructed its pupils that the President and his Administration in the executive branch made foreign policy and that the responsibility of the Congress, in the interest of bipartisanship, was to support the Administration's decisions. For example, when he used to go to the White House foreign policy briefings with Speaker Sam Rayburn,

Chairman Morgan remembers the Speaker saying to the President, "Now you tell us what you want the Congress to do, and we will do it."[118] This philosophy of bipartisan support for administrative decisions even carried over to congressional exercise of its constitutional power to declare war.

Rayburn's successor, John W. McCormack, followed this tradition of bipartisan cooperation in foreign policy. For example, in November 1969, McCormack, responding to White House requests, insisted that the Foreign Affairs Committee rush through a resolution applauding President Nixon's effort to achieve a just peace in Vietnam. Over the strong protest of some of his younger dovish committee members, Chairman Morgan reluctantly complied.

One day after the President's November 3, 1969, nationwide address on Vietnam, in which Nixon called on Americans to support his Vietnam withdrawal policy, the House introduced the resolution. It was actually drafted and circulated before the President's speech and sent to the White House for clearance. It endorsed President Nixon's efforts to achieve "peace with justice" in Vietnam and was the first major Vietnam policy declaration considered in the House since the Gulf of Tonkin Resolution in August 1964.[119]

Unlike Chairman Fulbright, the unassuming Chairman Morgan was known largely as a country doctor in western Pennsylvania. Affectionately called "Ole Doc" by his friends and colleagues around the Hill, his actions as chairman rarely made headlines. He disclaimed any interest in publicity for his work as chairman of the committee. However, one does not get to chair a House committee without some cunning and great political acuity. Despite maintaining a low-key profile, Morgan understood what Machiavelli advocated: that one must be shrewd to sustain leadership. He firmly believed "the initiative in foreign policy must be with the executive; as an objective evaluator of these initiatives, the Foreign Affairs Committee must approach them on a bipartisan basis and play mainly a subordinate role."[120]

Since their chairman sought to remain unassuming, the members of the House Foreign Affairs Committee did not try to upstage their leader. Despite their loyalty to "Ole Doc," in his subdued but disarming style, both Clement Zablocki (Wisconsin) and Dante Fascell (Florida), two ranking majority members of the committee, pointed out, "Doc has never restrained us [his subcommittee chairmen] in having a creative approach to foreign policy issues and ideas for implementation."[121]

Nevertheless, majority members of a committee generally reflected the decorum set by their chairman, and the House Foreign Affairs Committee of the 1960s and 1970s was no exception. The committee members mimicked the low-profile attitude of Chairman Morgan, just as Senate majority members of the Foreign Relations Committee—like Mansfield (Montana), Symington (Missouri), and McGovern (South Dakota)—seemed to prefer the headline-seeking approach of Chairman Fulbright. One cannot divorce the role of personalities from politics, and the personality of the Chairman indisputably sets the stylistic tone for the whole committee.

Likewise, the ideological or substance tone of a committee is often determined by the attitude of the Chairman. When considering the fourth question— *What was the ideological makeup of the Democrats on the House Foreign Affairs Committee?*—we look to its leader for the clues and confirm by judging committee action under his leadership. The answer: like its Chairman, the committee seemed to be rather hawkish.

Until the caucus action on April 20, 1972, Chairman Morgan, ranking Democratic members of the committee—such as Clement "Clem" Zablocki (Wisconsin) and Wayne Hays (Ohio)—and ranking Republican members—such as William Mailliard (California) and Peter Frelinghuysen (New Jersey)—were all hawks on Vietnam. Reflecting their chairman, Ole Doc Morgan, they had been successful in blocking consideration of any antiwar legislation by the committee. Morgan and these four top-ranking members of the committee had voted in 1971 against the Nedzi-Whalen (McGovern-Hatfield) and all Mansfield amendments.

Resolute and unwavering in his commitment to the House position on Vietnam in conferences with the Senate Foreign Relations Committee, Chairman Morgan had repeatedly refused to rescind and concur in any Senate amendments providing for termination of American involvement in Indochina by a date certain. This unflinching decision reflected the House position, since the House had consistently, time after time by 1972, voted down these Senate amendments.[122] Moreover, Morgan represented the majority of the House's position on the Vietnam issue. (Remember, the House had never passed any kind of end-the-war legislation prior to 1972.)

The importance of the Chairman of the Committee in deciding what type and in what form legislation will be reported by his committee cannot be underestimated. It is the Chairman's prerogative to determine when legislation will be considered by the committee, to approve the scheduling of hearings on the legislation, and to control the number and kinds of witnesses who will testify on behalf of or against a measure. The Chairman can easily stack the witnesses in support of a particular point of view, as Chairman Fulbright so often did throughout the late 1960s during the consideration of measures such as the Vietnam resolutions. His tactics seemed to work in the Senate Foreign Relations Committee . . . only to die in the House Foreign Affairs Committee at the end of each congressional term.

Doc Morgan was naturally considered a Democratic Party regular. "Party regulars" may be liberal, moderate, or conservative in ideology, but they put the good of the party above their personal ideology and stay constant to the party leadership. Like O'Neill, Morgan was a popular member of the House and, like all other committee chairmen, a staunch defendant of the seniority system, which was coming increasingly under attack by the newly elected doves, who were almost always issue-oriented liberals.

Obviously, Doc Morgan did not look kindly upon these liberal upstarts who openly attacked the very system by which the doctor was able to become chairman of the Foreign Affairs Committee. Ever since 1970, when a majority of these members, all outspoken doves on the Vietnam polemic, were first elected to the Congress, they had vigorously importuned Chairman Morgan to hold hearings on Vietnam. Specifically, they attempted to pressure the committee into introducing privileged resolutions seeking confidential and classified information concerning the war from the Pentagon and State Department.

As one of these issue-oriented liberals, the vocal Bella Abzug (New York) was among the most frequent antagonists on the war issue. Today hailed as an equal rights defendant and social activist, she was considered then by many members of Congress, Democrat and Republican, as overly abrasive and even appallingly "unladylike" in manner. She was aggressive, she seldom minced words—she even swore—and many male members did not respond favorably to her confrontational style.

Doc Morgan always seemed to delight in seeing Representative Abzug defeated on the floor of the House. For instance, some members[123] swore they saw a gleeful look on Doc Morgan's face one day when the House was in session for floor votes. Barely two minutes after the House had convened at noon that day, Doc Morgan rose quickly to be recognized by the Speaker. At once, he motioned to table Abzug's demand for certain documents from the Pentagon pertaining to the war. In a swift vote, her motion was laid on the table (killed) before she could even reach the House floor to object!

However, like the Speaker and Majority Leader, who were also longtime supporters of Johnson's and

Nixon's management of the war, Doc Morgan had also become somewhat dissatisfied with Nixon's conduct of the Vietnamization process while simultaneously expanding American involvement in the air war throughout Indochina. Despite his long-standing and solid hawkish position on Vietnam, Chairman Morgan was, as he said, "first a Democrat." As such, he felt bound by the action of the Democratic caucus on April 20.

Although no chairman likes to have his committee mandated by his party's caucus to take legislative action, Morgan fully intended to abide by the caucus action and to report out end-the-war legislation within thirty days. Be that as it may, what could not be known was *how* he intended to report legislation and if his heart was truly set on ending the war.

CHAPTER 11

Thirty-Day Deadline

Democratic members of the House Foreign Affairs Committee, under Doc Morgan's leadership, would decide the committee's response to O'Neill's caucus resolution. This leads to question number five: How did the members view their committee role in foreign policy determination, in particular the Vietnam War? The answer to that question lies in the issue of party loyalty, which had much to do with personal convictions. Who among the committee Democratic members were party regulars, and who were issue-oriented liberals? How many hawks were on the committee, and how many doves?

The Democratic composition of the committee hawks and doves in 1972 provides an interesting study in diversity. Clement Zablocki, ranking Democratic member after Morgan, was chairman of the Subcommittee on National Security Policy and Scientific Development. Also, he was one of the leading hawks on the House Foreign Affairs Committee.

Short, stout, and Polish, Zablocki was an affable and well-liked member of Congress, representing a strong Democratic district of Polish-German Milwaukee, Wisconsin. He was very close to Chairman Morgan and, in fact, to the whole Pennsylvania congressional delegation, with whom he always sat in the House chamber. Considered a party regular, Zablocki had been an outspoken hawk on the war and a firm supporter of Nixon's Vietnamization policy. One of the zone whips and personally very fond of O'Neill, Zablocki had nonetheless been a consistent opponent of the Majority Whip whenever the issue of Vietnam came up.

However, following the Cambodian incursion in May 1970, Zablocki took the initiative to investigate the war-making powers of the President, which had become his favorite legislative project. After eleven days of hearings, his subcommittee approved a resolution, which required the President to submit to Congress a written report when he committed U.S. armed forces without prior congressional authorization. It also called upon the President "whenever feasible" to seek "appropriate consultation" with Congress before involving American forces in armed conflict abroad.[124] (It was believed to be the genesis of the War Powers Act, which would be enacted by Congress in 1973.)

This novel Zablocki resolution, which passed the House, put that chamber on record as insisting that it, too, had a part to play in American foreign policy. Chairman Zablocki used his position as subcommittee chairman to shepherd member support to report out of his subcommittee an unprecedented resolution. He wanted to ensure that when the House Committee challenged the Administration on American commitments overseas, including Southeast Asia, it challenged in a responsible way.

Zablocki believed the Senate Cooper-Church and McGovern-Hatfield amendments of pullout dates and restrictions of funds for American activities in Southeast Asia obstructed Administration policy and tied its hands. Rather, his subcommittee probed the constitutional prerogatives of the executive-legislative branches on war-making decisions through hearings and a resolution. It was a markedly different approach from O'Neill's caucus resolution. The Majority Whip was utilizing, not probing, the constitutional power of the legislative branch to terminate U.S. military action in Vietnam.

"The Senate Foreign Relations Committee is hell-bent to get out of Vietnam," Zablocki said, "but they [the members of that committee] will give anything to the Middle East. . . . I know that Fulbright said my resolution was wishy-washy . . . but . . . I have every confidence that the President got the message."[125]

At one whip coffee meeting late in 1971, during a discussion of one of the Mansfield amendments, Clem Zablocki blurted out sarcastically, "Well, if I had the radical college constituency Tip does, I guess I'd be against the war too." Immediately, Tip O'Neill challenged Zablocki, pointing out emphatically and not without considerable emotion that his position on Vietnam was a matter of personal conviction.

He had undergone a transition in early 1967, when he began to hear the other side of the issue from leading members of the military establishment who spoke to him confidentially and off the record. These Pentagon officials expressed their personal reservations about American involvement in the Vietnam conflict. The Harvard-MIT element in his constituency had absolutely no influence on his Vietnam position, O'Neill asserted.[126]

Indeed, O'Neill's support came from the Irish and Italian Americans on the back streets of Boston and North Cambridge, not from the Ivy League intelligentsia. After altering his position in 1967, O'Neill had to educate his "back-street" people to his new position. In no way did his constituency influence his stance. Though O'Neill explained his position at great length to Zablocki and the rest of the whips at that coffee meeting, it was obvious to all who were present that Zablocki remained unconvinced.

Consequently, the day after the April 20 caucus, it was not surprising to O'Neill when Zablocki informed him that, regardless of his personal affection for Tip, he intended to fight the O'Neill resolution all the way, both in the committee and on the floor. In addition, Wayne Hays (Ohio), another outstanding committee hawk, let O'Neill know that he would also not be bound in committee by the O'Neill caucus resolution.

After Zablocki, Hays was the next ranking majority member of the committee and chairman of the Committee on House Administration. He was considered a party regular, a hawk on Vietnam, and a hardliner on communism.

"We should bomb the hell out of those no-good Commie bastards," he once said.[127] Perhaps the meanest, most vindictive man in the Congress, Hays did not care who he offended. He would lash out at a member, a staff person, a floor employee—even a foreign government—with a poker face and a total lack of empathy.

Reliable sources[128] on the Foreign Affairs Committee insist that the idea of suspending aid to Greece nine months previously in 1971 originated with Wayne Hays. They said Hays was indignant because the Greek government did not give him the "red carpet" treatment when he visited the country earlier that year. He decided that if they did not know how to show their appreciation to a ranking member of the Foreign Affairs Committee, which was the House committee responsible for granting economic and military assistance to Greece, then the Greeks did not deserve any more aid.

Of course, Hays overlooked the point that perhaps the reason for the cool treatment he received in Greece resulted from his vituperative blasts condemning the Greek regime—remarks that he made quite frequently on the House floor. In any case, Wayne Hays decided that Greece did not deserve any U.S. financial or military assistance. And because of the power he wielded as chairman of the House Administration Committee, he was able to convince his colleagues on the committee and the Democratic leadership in the House that aid should be suspended to Greece until the country returned to a constitutional democracy.

Many members feared Wayne Hays. He had established for himself a potentate as chairman of the House Administration Committee, a committee that under his aegis had taken on jurisdiction that overlapped several other committees, as well as the offices of the Clerk and the Doorkeeper. A fierce and pugnacious orator, he instilled fear in the few members who dared to take him on during floor debate of specific legislation. If any members did challenge him on the House floor, Hays made them look so marginalized that they usually did not speak out for weeks after their verbal shellacking from Hays.[129]

Where did O'Neill's resolution stand with these top-ranking Democratic members? Although Doc Morgan publicly *said* he would follow the caucus directive, O'Neill knew for certain that Zablocki and Hays would be contrary.

Dante Fascell (Florida), another ranking member of the Foreign Affairs Committee, was chairman of the Subcommittee on Inter-American Affairs. Since becoming chairman of that subcommittee in 1969, Fascell had held impressive investigatory hearings on the whole range of U.S. relations with her Latin American neighbors. Most noticeable were his investigatory hearings in 1971 on U.S. negotiations with the Panamanian government over a new treaty regarding jurisdiction in the Panama Canal Zone. When Fascell learned that the Administration had entered negotiations to facilitate a change in the governance of the Canal Zone, Fascell's subcommittee held four days of hearings. The purpose: to uncover the main objective of the U.S. negotiators, which was to turn over much of the administration of the Canal Zone to the Panamanians.

The subcommittee hearings sought to inform the Administration of congressional concern over these changes. Members of the Democratic House leadership, including Majority Whip O'Neill, even participated in the hearings and held informal briefings with chief U.S. negotiator, Ambassador John C. Mundt. It was Fascell's subcommittee that fostered the whole concept of social development assistance, which grew out of Title IX of the Inter-American Development provision of the foreign aid program.[130]

Short, gregarious, and Italian, Dante Fascell represented the heavily Jewish district of Miami, Florida. Though classified as a party regular, Fascell was an integral part of the Gibbons "New South" group. An advisor and close confidant to Sam Gibbons, he was involved in that abortive strategic and procedural attempt in the caucus to force a vote on the Gibbons amendment before a vote could be taken on the O'Neill resolution. If successful, it would have precluded a vote on the O'Neill resolution. But Fascell liked and respected O'Neill, and in committee, he would be behind a strong antiwar measure 100 percent.

Significantly, for a committee that had been dominated by hawks, including Doc Morgan himself, each new subcommittee chairman elected after 1970 had identified with the antiwar element in the House. The Legislative Reorganization Act of 1970 prohibited a member from being chairman of more than one subcommittee. The purpose of the reform was to spread the chair responsibilities around so that junior members could obtain a subcommittee chairmanship. It opened up leadership opportunities for younger and more liberal Democratic members, who were often doves. Women benefited as well. As an increasing number of women were elected to the House in later decades, more and more subcommittee chairs eventually became open to them.

Although no women served on the Foreign Affairs Committee, much less the prestigious Rules or Appropriations Committees, one woman served on the Ways and Means Committee—Martha Griffiths (Michigan). She was a long-serving, well-respected, knowledgeable, and conscientious member. She always did her homework, worked hard, and moved up through the seniority ranks as a party regular.

The Legislative Reform Act was the key reform achieved by the DSG in its early years. For instance, the newly elected chairman of the Foreign Affairs' Subcommittee on International Organization was the issue-oriented liberal Donald Fraser (Minnesota), a past chairman of the Democratic Study Group. Fraser used his subcommittee to scrutinize Administration programs closely.

"Taking the executive on faith was a mistake, particularly on Vietnam. Now I don't believe much of what I am told," said Fraser.[131]

A close political ally of Drinan, Abzug, Burton, and other issue-oriented liberals, Fraser would be unwilling to compromise on the issue of Vietnam. And in committee he would support the strongest proposal for termination of American involvement.

One of Fraser's colleagues on the committee was Lee Hamilton, the newly elected chairman of the Subcommittee on the Near East, which was concerned primarily with Palestinian refugees. When asked once about the House Committee vis-à-vis its Senate counterpart, Hamilton said, "We've got to be more assertive. We've all experienced being asked, 'Where the hell were you guys?'"[132]

Hamilton, a zone whip from Indiana and personally close to fellow Indianan John Brademas, the Assistant Majority Whip, was a quiet, resourceful, and thoughtful party regular, yet an unequivocal dove on Vietnam. He believed that the drive for a much more critical examination of foreign policy by the House Committee would evolve from public disenchantment with Vietnam.

He said, "We [the House Foreign Affairs Committee] ought to produce the finest work in the country. The Committee should be the focal point for the best thinking on foreign policy."[133]

Benjamin Rosenthal, who headed the European subcommittee, was an issue-oriented liberal, a member of the DSG, and a member of the liberal New York delegation, consisting of Shirley Chisholm, John Bingham, Bella Abzug, Ed Koch, Herman Badillo, and Rosenthal. No one would second-guess his reasons for being a dove on Vietnam.

John Culver, new chairman of the Subcommittee on Foreign Economic Policy, a former football player and aide to Sen. Edward Kennedy, was a popular, issue-oriented liberal from Iowa. His dovish stand on Vietnam was unquestioned.

L. H. Fountain (North Carolina), John Davis (Georgia), and Roy Taylor (North Carolina) were all conservative Southern members of the committee who had supported unequivocally the President, Democrat or Republican, in his conduct of foreign policy. None of the three would ever consider voting for a congressional initiative to determine the duration of America's involvement in Indochina. Like Zablocki and Hays, they felt unbound by the caucus instructions to the Democratic members of the Foreign Affairs Committee.

Three members of the Congressional Black Caucus were also on the House Foreign Affairs Committee. Although not as numerous or powerful then, the CBC is very influential today, with fifty-six members "committed to using the full Constitutional power, statutory authority, and financial resources of the federal government to ensure that African Americans and other marginalized communities in the United States have the opportunity to achieve the American Dream."[134] In fact, the current House majority whip and the highest-ranking House member of color, James E. "Jim" Clyburn (South Carolina), is a member of the CBC.

But back in 1971, the CBC was founded by thirteen members of Congress, three of which served on the Foreign Affairs Committee in 1972. Although different in personality and philosophy, all three were doves on the war issue and would support the caucus resolution.

Robert Nelson Cornelius Nix Sr. (Pennsylvania), the eldest and most senior of the three, was a party regular. Very close to his colleague from Pennsylvania, Chairman Morgan, and to Clem Zablocki, he took his usual seat on the House floor with the Pennsylvania delegation in the far back row on the right side of the House chamber. Unassuming and quiet, Nix was probably the most conservative member of the Black Caucus.

Charles Coles Diggs Jr. (Michigan), chairman of the Subcommittee on African Affairs and the ranking member of the District (Washington, D.C.) Committee (he would become its chairman in the 93rd Congress), was a moderate, issue-oriented liberal and former chairman of the Congressional Black Caucus. Aggressive, conscientious, and resourceful, he had traveled widely, making several trips to Africa since he came to Congress, and he was well respected by the House leadership and party regulars.

Ronald V. Dellums, a first-term congressman from Berkeley, California, personified well his constituency as an unrelenting and strident antiwar dove. The lowest-ranking Democrat on the committee, Dellums was outspoken, an issue-oriented liberal à la Drinan, and extremely Black-conscious. The conservative, Southern, white establishment in the House considered Dellums militant, dangerous, and uncompromising.

At the time, Dellums was not very well received by the House Democratic leadership. He often expressed the view that all legislative issues could be reduced to a racial denominator. Unafraid to say what needed to be said, Dellums was known to get up during a legislative debate on the House floor and attack all white members present in the chamber as "racists." Today, Dellums would probably fit in as one of the progressive Democrats. But that kind of behavior in the 92nd Congress did not augur well with the Southern-controlled House of Representatives, not to mention some white ethnic-oriented Northerners.

Issue-oriented or party regular, all three CBC members would no doubt lend a hand in policy that would potentially end the war.

Three other New Yorkers on the committee—Lester Wolff, Jonathan Bingham, and Ogden Reid—were all issue-oriented liberals and members of the DSG. Reid, a maverick and renegade Republican, had just changed his party affiliation to Democrat early in 1972. The other New Yorker, Seymour "Sy" Halpern, was one of the most liberal Republicans serving in the House. All four would support strong end-the-war committee action.

The notorious Cornelius Gallagher (New Jersey) was still seated on the House Foreign Affairs Committee. He was in more legal trouble in that allegedly "corrupt" state of New Jersey than any one man could possibly combat head-on. Nevertheless, he confronted multiple charges of extortion, embezzlement, alleged Mafia connections, campaign fraud, and misuse of funds. Already he had been indicted by a New Jersey grand jury and would face certain conviction. Since the illegal disclosures had hit the press, Gallagher's attendance record had dropped considerably. Political survival was no longer a question; he was now fighting to save himself from a long prison term. His personal problems were far more important than concern over an end-the-war resolution.

Four other party regulars—none of whom were leading opponents of the war, but all of whom would support the position of Chairman Morgan—rounded out the Democratic membership of the Foreign Affairs Committee: Constantine "Gus" Yatron (Ohio), discreet and unassuming; John Monagan (Connecticut), quiet, able, and talented; Abraham "Chick" Kazen (Texas); and Morgan Murphy (Illinois), an integral part of Mayor Daley's Chicago delegation in the House and very close pal of Dan Rostenkowski, the leader of the Chicago delegation and later chairman of the powerful House Ways and Means Committee.

***

Now, back to the first question: Would the committee report out legislation favorable to the O'Neill caucus directive? The outlook seemed hopeful. Even though the past committee action tended to reflect the hawkish opinion of its chairman, Morgan's mind was changing, and the committee's Democratic makeup leaned more toward the dovish position. It appeared as if the five—Zablocki, Hays, Fountain, Davis, and Taylor—would be the only uncompromising Democratic hawks on the Vietnam issue in spite of the caucus mandate.

For the O'Neill caucus resolution had mandated all twenty-two Democrats on the House Foreign Affairs Committee to perform two functions:

1. Prepare legislation terminating all U.S. military involvement in and over Indochina by a date certain, subject only to obtaining release of American prisoners of war and all available information on the missing in action; and
2. Report that legislation for House action within 30 days (i.e., by May 20, 1972).[135]

In order to comply with this required directive, the Democrats on the committee had to proceed differently from the way they would have considered a bill under normal circumstances. First, they needed to assemble and prepare a measure (a bill, resolution, or amendment to a bill) following the dictates of the O'Neill resolution. Then, whatever the majority decided upon had to be supported in committee by all twenty-two Democratic members.

This meant that the Democratic members should attend all meetings, at which there might be votes on the measure, or else give their proxy to the leader of the Democratic majority on the committee. It meant they should oppose all amendments not agreed to by the majority of Democrats on the committee. It also meant they should vote to report the measure for House consideration, even though they might oppose it later on the House floor.

These minimal requirements, however, did not preclude dissenting Democratic members of the committee from other activities, provided such other activities did not prevent or hinder the majority of Democrats on the committee from complying with the directives of the caucus. Thus, dissenting Democrats would be free to voice their views, offer amendments, file dissenting views as part of the committee report, and recommend that the measure be amended or defeated by the full House.

In addition, when the measure was considered in the House, any Democratic member of the committee would be free to vote against it, as well as offer amendments and oppose it verbally. But while it was in committee, each Democratic member was required to make his vote available and cast it in accord with the wishes of the majority of Democrats on the committee.[136]

To accomplish this objective, the committee was under extreme pressure. It had merely thirty days to report out a measure for House floor action. But even then, Congress more frequently than not failed to meet its prescribed deadlines, even when the matter was of utmost urgency.

Lay It on the Table

CHAPTER 12

A Committee Deliberates

The Foreign Affairs Committee had thirty days in which to act on the O'Neill-Gibbons caucus resolution. Twenty days elapsed without any committee action.

Meanwhile, the action in Vietnam ramped up. On May 8, President Nixon announced the mining and blockade of the Haiphong Harbor and other North Vietnamese ports, much to the disbelief, chagrin, and consternation of the doves in Congress.[137]

Two days later, on May 10, the Democratic members of the Foreign Affairs Committee met in an executive session, without the presence of any reporters or the public. At that meeting, junior committee member Lee Hamilton (Indiana) put forth a resolution as the committee response to the O'Neill directive from the Democratic caucus.

Hamilton's resolution read:

Notwithstanding any provision of this or any other Act, the involvement of United States land, sea, and air forces, for the purpose of maintaining, supporting, or engaging in hostilities in or over Indochina, shall terminate and such forces shall be withdrawn not later than October 1, 1972, subject to a cease-fire between the United States and North Vietnam and those allied with North Vietnam to the extent necessary to achieve safe withdrawal of such remaining forces, and subject to the release of all American prisoners of war held by the Government of North Vietnam and forces allied with that government.[138]

A majority of the Democrats on the committee who were in attendance at the executive session endorsed Hamilton's proposal, which, with the Chairman's support, quickly became known as the Morgan-Hamilton provision.

So it was that while the Democrat members of the House Foreign Affairs Committee met to consider legislation that would bring about a termination of American involvement in the war, the President attended a summit conference in Moscow. Ostensibly, the summit seemed unhampered, and perhaps even strengthened, by Nixon's aggressive actions in Indochina. Neither China nor Russia openly challenged President Nixon's blockade.

Additionally, at the May 10 executive session, Zablocki offered his own resolution to provide for the termination of hostilities in Indochina, which he submitted after the introduction of Hamilton's proposal. His resolution read as follows:

Resolved by the Senate and House of Representatives of the United States of America in Congress assembled, that the involvement of U.S. military forces, land, sea or air, for the purpose of maintaining, supporting, or engaging in hostilities in or over Indochina shall terminate and such forces shall be withdrawn not later than 3 months following the establishment of a cease-fire to assure the safe withdrawal of such forces and subject to the release of all prisoners of war held by the Government of North Vietnam and forces allied with such government and an accounting for all Americans missing in action who have been held by or known to such Government or such forces. The accounting for the American prisoners of war and missing in action referred to above shall be subject to verification by the International Red Cross or any other international body mutually agreed to by the President of the U.S. and the Government of North Vietnam.[139]

The resolution offered by Clement Zablocki was identical to the President's proposal: withdrawal of all U.S. forces from Vietnam, conditional upon (1) an internationally supervised cease-fire throughout all Indochina, (2) return of American prisoners of war, and (3) accounting of MIAs. The Morgan-Hamilton proposal, however, called for a simultaneous cease-fire among the combatants—the United States, North Vietnam, and Viet Cong[140]—only to the extent necessary for the withdrawal of U.S. troops and the safe return of POWs.

It was the condition of the cease-fire that was the crucial difference between the Morgan-Hamilton proposal and the Zablocki design. Unlike the original Drinan bill, H.R. 14055, the Morgan-Hamilton proposal did not cut off all funds for American ground and air military operations in and over Indochina within thirty days of enactment. It merely set a date certain—October 1, 1972—for termination of American military involvement subject to the release of American POWs. On the other hand, Zablocki's proposal set a nebulous date of "not later than three months following the establishment of a cease-fire" for termination of hostilities. Since Zablocki's resolution was in effect the President's proposal, it was dead on arrival at the Democratic executive session.

Following the executive meeting of the Democratic members of the Foreign Affairs Committee, in which they endorsed the Morgan-Hamilton proposal by voice vote, Doc Morgan seemed in no hurry to call a full meeting on the Vietnam proposal. One month later, on June 10, O'Neill importuned Morgan to follow through on the caucus directive. Three days later, the full committee met in executive session, at which Morgan offered the Democratic resolution.

Since the Zablocki proposal had been scuttled by the Democratic members one month before, Republican Representative John Buchanan (Alabama) submitted the President's proposal as a substitute to the Morgan-Hamilton resolution. It read:

That it is the sense of the Congress that at a time certain, not later than four months following the establishment of an internationally supervised cease-fire throughout Indochina and the return of all American prisoners of war and an accounting of all Americans missing in action in Indochina, a complete withdrawal of all American forces from Vietnam shall be accomplished.[141]

Essentially, Buchanan's resolution was Zablocki's resolution with its condition for withdrawal based on the concept of an internationally supervised cease-fire. The Buchanan substitute was nothing more than a restatement of the President's program for withdrawal of all American forces from Indochina. It set no date certain, except a nebulous four-month window of withdrawal following an internationally supervised cease-fire. The stronger, more emphatic and specific Democratic version, the Morgan-Hamilton proposal, set a definite date, calling for a withdrawal of all American involvement from Indochina by October 1, 1972.

The first vote by the committee was on the Buchanan substitute. It carried by one vote, 19 to 18. The breakdown on the Buchanan substitute was as follows:[142]

Democrats For:	Republicans For:
1. Clement Zablocki (Wisconsin)	1. William Mailliard (California)
2. Wayne Hays (Ohio)	2. Peter Frelinghuysen (New Jersey)

Democrats For:	Republicans For:
3. L. H. Fountain (North Carolina)	3. William Broomfield (Michigan)
4. Roy Taylor (North Carolina)	4. Irving Whalley (Pennsylvania)
5. John Davis (Georgia)	5. H. R. Gross (Iowa)
	6. Edward Derwinski (Illinois)
	7. Vernon Thomson (Wisconsin)
	8. Paul Findley (Illinois)
	9. John Buchanan (Alabama)
	10. Sherman Lloyd (Utah)
	11. Herbert Burke (Florida)
	12. Guy Vander Jagt (Michigan)
	13. Pierres du Pont (Delaware)
	14. Robert Mathias (California)

Democrats Against:	Republicans Against:
1. Thomas Morgan (Pennsylvania)	1. Robert Steele (Connecticut)
2. Dante Fascell (Florida)	2. Charles Whalen (Ohio)
3. Charles Diggs (Michigan)	
4. Robert Nix (Pennsylvania)	
5. John Monagan (Connecticut)	

Democrats Against:	Republicans Against:
6. Donald Fraser (Minnesota)	
7. Benjamin Rosenthal (New York)	
8. John Culver (Iowa)	
9. Lee Hamilton (Indiana)	
10. Abraham Kazen (Texas)	
11. Lester Wolff (New York)	
12. Jonathan Bingham (New York)	
13. Gus Yatron (Pennsylvania)	
14. Morgan Murphy (Illinois)	
15. Ronald Dellums (California)	
16. Ogden Reid (New York)	

Democrats Absent:	Republicans Absent:
1. Cornelius Gallagher (New Jersey)	1. Seymour Halpern (New York)

With a ratio of twenty-two Democrats to seventeen Republicans on the committee, the Democratic version should have prevailed. But Gallagher and Halpern had missed the vote. Both would have voted against the Buchanan resolution, thus making the vote 19 to 20 for a defeat of the substitute.

Gallagher, so enmeshed in legal difficulty, was in New Jersey preparing his defense for the upcoming trial. His Washington staff had failed to notify him of the morning executive session. Even if they had, it was unlikely that he would have been present for the vote. Halpern arrived at the committee room just minutes too late to cast a vote. He had been "detained in a Rayburn corridor by two Republicans from New York."[143]

The issue-oriented liberals on the committee—particularly Fraser, Culver, Rosenthal, Reid, and Dellums—were outraged by the vote on the Buchanan substitute. They focused their anger and disregard of party loyalty on the five Democrats who had voted for the Buchanan substitute. Unquestionably, Zablocki, Hays, Fountain, Taylor, and Davis had violated the caucus directive. The majority of the Democrats who had met in executive session on May 10 had supported, by voice vote, the Morgan-Hamilton resolution. In other words, the Democrats had rejected Zablocki's version, which was an endorsement of the President's program for disengagement.

According to the implication of the caucus directive—which was clearly interpreted by the doves to bind all Democratic members of the Foreign Affairs Committee to support the Morgan-Hamilton version in full committee—they were obliged to oppose any amendment or substitute, such as Buchanan's, which was not supported by the majority of Democrats on the committee. All Democratic members were required to have voted unanimously to report out the Morgan-Hamilton resolution for House consideration, even though some of them might later oppose it on the House floor. The caucus directive had implied that

Democratic members of the committee should attend all meetings at which there might be votes on the bill, or else give their proxy to the Chairman. Gallagher did not do that. So, the Buchanan resolution prevailed in committee because two antiwar members were absent (one Democrat and one Republican) and five Democrats refused to be bound in committee by the caucus directive.

Was there any evidence of collaboration between Zablocki and Buchanan, since Zablocki was so vigorously opposed to the Morgan-Hamilton end-the-war provision? All evidence attainable indicates that no plot existed between the two congressmen. As Fascell pointed out, "There was no reason for collaboration. Every Democrat on the committee knew that a Republican substitute would be offered to represent the President's position. What really shocked the younger, liberal members of the committee was that Zablocki and Hays, the two top-ranking Democrats on the committee, would support in committee the Republican substitute, considering the directive from the caucus."[144]

Buchanan summed up the reasons for adoption of his substitute in remarks to reporters, which appeared in *The Washington Post*:

Public opinion in the United States has rallied to the President's support. Therefore, it was quite logical that the majority of the Committee adopt a resolution which is a basic endorsement of the President's peace proposal . . . rather than the original resolution ordered by the Democratic Caucus: We commend the statesmanship and courage of those Democratic members who stood with the majority of Republicans in support of this resolution which would strengthen the President's hand at the negotiating table.[145]

In the same piece, Zablocki explained the reasons why he could not support the Morgan-Hamilton version:

The directive from the Caucus was to report out within 30 days legislation which meets the objective of termination of American involvement in Indochina, safe withdrawal of our troops and return of POWs. The Morgan-Hamilton version makes no effort to end the fighting in Southeast Asia—it seeks simply to end U.S. participation in the conflict. Such a formula should it be accepted by the enemy would virtually assure a continuation of the fighting—an objective which we surely do not seek. This provision, furthermore, is unlikely to secure the release of American POWs since it does not meet Hanoi's principal demand that we overthrow Thieu and cease all aid to the government of South Vietnam.[146]

Lee Hamilton, who had originally introduced the Democratic version, was especially perturbed over the vote. He told reporters, "This is nothing more than an endorsement of the President's program for disengagement from Vietnam. I can't believe the sell-out by some of my Democratic colleagues who supported the Buchanan substitute."[147]

In the press conference, Doc Morgan came to the rescue, defending Zablocki's action: "Look, the Vietnam war issue is a matter of deep, personal conviction to Clem. Knowing his position on the cease-fire condition, I don't think he could have voted in good conscience any other way."[148]

When Thomas P. O'Neill learned of the committee's adoption of the Buchanan substitute, which most closely approximated the policy of the President, he said privately on the floor to his legislative assistant, "Well, at least we got something to work with from the committee."[149]

Despite this voiced optimism, O'Neill was inwardly skeptical. As a legislative leader, he knew how to outwardly camouflage doubts, think and act positively, and sound upbeat. But given Morgan's past support of the President's Vietnamization process, O'Neill was suspicious of the Chairman's commitment to the caucus directive. To reporters, O'Neill pointed out that the resolution could be amended on the floor if Chairman Morgan asked for an open rule. Then the Morgan-Hamilton proposal would be offered as a substitute.[150]

The committee action on the Buchanan substitute illustrates a part of the standard legislative process in action. For example, the Democratic members had caucused on May 10 and endorsed by voice vote the Morgan-Hamilton proposal. A month later, the full committee met again in executive session (no public or reporters present) to deliberate on two legislative proposals that had been introduced by members of the committee. A vote was taken; the Buchanan substitute prevailed.

According to a staff member, there was no real deliberation: "Everyone knew the issues involved. Everyone knew that the crucial differences between the Republican and Democratic plans for disengagement were the cease-fire provision and date certain. Minds were made up beforehand. At the June 13th meeting, it was just a question of recording the votes."[151]

The Morgan-Hamilton proposal would have been the appropriate answer to the caucus directive. Yet the committee, by a one-vote margin, ordered reported on June 13 H.J.Res. 1225, the Buchanan resolution. All this because two members were absent and five refused to be bound in committee by the caucus action.

Yes, the Foreign Affairs Committee had acted; yet it had not acted resolutely. The Morgan-Hamilton resolution had been preliminarily and narrowly defeated in committee. In essence, it was laid on the legislative table, but only temporarily—not killed. It would be revisited by the Foreign Affairs Committee.

Although, on June 13, the Buchanan resolution was ordered reported by the House Foreign Affairs Committee, the report was never filed. Why not? Early in June, the committee had begun hearings on the 1972 foreign aid authorization bill, which was the major annual legislative responsibility of the House Committee. Following completion of those hearings in July, the committee began marking up the bill.

Prior to the first markup session, Hamilton spoke to Morgan about offering his end-the-war resolution as a committee amendment. Unlike the situation in June when the Buchanan substitute won because two members—Gallagher and Halpern—were absent, Hamilton reasoned that all committee Democrats would be in attendance for the markup on the foreign aid bill. If all the Democratic members of the committee were present at the markup, his committee amendment would prevail.

Morgan eagerly complied with Hamilton's request. The Morgan-Hamilton resolution was attached to the foreign aid bill in markup as a committee amendment by a vote of 19 to 17.[152] The Morgan-Hamilton provision became Section 13 in the bill. Neither Morgan nor Hamilton at the time thought to change the date, even though many weeks had passed since the first draft of their resolution.

When the Foreign Affairs Committee reported the foreign aid bill on August 1, Section 13 contained the original October 1 deadline for termination of American involvement in Indochina. Recall that the October deadline came from the attempt on May 10 by the Democratic members of the committee to write a resolution mandating a withdrawal deadline in response to the directive from the April caucus. Therefore, when the Foreign Affairs Committee drafted the foreign aid bill nearly three months later, it picked up the old May 10th provision but neglected to change the date.

Now that it was already August, October 1 was less than two months away. Moreover, Congress was going into a three-week recess for the Republican Convention, from August 18 until after Labor Day, September 5.

Meanwhile, the Senate had yet to revive the foreign aid bill, which it had killed on July 24 by a vote of 48 to 42.[153] Senate doves had succeeded in adding both a mandatory cutoff of funds for the war and a flat, binding, end-the-war amendment, furthering the efforts of Mansfield and Fulbright the previous year. Senators against the war had managed to write legislation that would discontinue the seemingly endless Vietnamization process by not only tightening the purse strings but also tying a knot in them. While it sounded like a victory for the doves, it was nothing more than a pyrrhic victory for them. Without enough support for such a strict proposal, the foreign assistance bill was doomed in the Senate. Renewal of the foreign assistance authorization was major legislation for the Congress every few years. The Senate could not let the authorization expire; it would have to revive the bill.

Since the foreign aid bill had to be voted on by the full House, and a revived Senate version had yet to be reconsidered in that chamber, time was running out. Most likely, the revived Senate bill would differ from the bill passed by the House, thus forcing a Senate-House conference. Who knew how long this would go on? Weeks surely, but months more likely. The October 1 deadline was not only impractical—it was totally unrealistic.

Representative Charles Whalen (Ohio), a liberal Republican member of the House Foreign Affairs Committee, was a supporter of end-the-war opportunities and voted in committee against the Buchanan amendment. He had been elected to Congress in 1966 and had served in WWII as an army officer in the Far East. From that experience, he "developed very strong reservations" at first, then opposition to the Vietnam War.[154] Like O'Neill, he could not justify the war's sacrifices to his constituents, especially parents grieving the loss of their young Marine son. Once he opposed the Vietnam War, he wanted to end the conflict. He took great pride in co-sponsoring with his friend and Democratic colleague Lucien Nedzi (Michigan) the Nedzi-Whalen amendment to end military funding to prolong the war.

Whalen desired to make the Morgan-Hamilton proposal bipartisan. He asked Morgan, and received the Chairman's full support, to intervene with an amendment on the House floor that would change the withdrawal deadline from October 1 to December 31. This amendment became known as the Morgan-Hamilton-Whalen proposal.

One other Republican member of the Foreign Affairs Committee, Robert Steele (Connecticut), supported an end to the Vietnam War, joining Whalen in opposition to the Buchanan amendment. Steele, a freshman House member in the 92nd Congress, was elected in a special election after the death of his predecessor, William St. Onge, a Democrat.

In light of delayed congressional action on the bill and the necessity of a conference between the two chambers, the Whalen amendment would give the Nixon Administration until the end of the year to withdraw American troops from Vietnam. Additionally, by setting a date at the end of December, after the presidential election and adjournment of Congress, the House would remove the issue from the political arena.

However necessary, the change of date from an October 1 to a December 31 deadline was to be the tragic flaw that would split the war critics.

CHAPTER 13

✿

A Tale of Two Dates: Section 13 and the Whalen Amendment

At 9:15 on Thursday morning, August 3, 1972, at the weekly whip coffee, Majority Leader Hale Boggs announced the schedule of House floor legislation for the week of August 7. The Speaker, Majority Leader, Chairman of the Democratic caucus, and the twenty zone whips from across the country gathered in the whip office to discuss the specifics of the next week's legislative schedule, prepared by the Majority Leader's office, and the Democratic leadership position on these items.

In addition to scheduling legislation, Majority Leader Boggs acted as primary spokesman for the House Democrats. Often, the Leader would close the floor debate for the majority on a measure that was of special importance to the Democrats and which usually had been subjected to a whip count. A fine, extemporaneous orator, it was in his position as spokesman for the Democratic Party in the House that Hale Boggs excelled.

When the Majority Leader decided to put a bill on the docket for floor consideration, he had to first check with the committee chairman who had jurisdiction over the bill, as well as the Chairman of the Rules Committee, if it was a non-appropriation matter, to determine the House floor procedure for consideration of the bill. Hence, he had done his homework on the foreign aid bill.

With the approval of House Foreign Affairs Committee Chairman Morgan and Rules Committee Chairman William Colmer (Mississippi), Hale Boggs announced at that August 3rd whip coffee that H.R. 16029, the Foreign Assistance Act of 1972, would be scheduled for House floor consideration on August 8, 9, and 10. The Rules Committee had already held a hearing on the bill and had recommended an open rule (amendments could be offered) with three hours of general debate on the merits of the bill.[155]

As Boggs read the schedule, he pointed out that the leadership planned to debate only on Tuesday the 8th, to read for amendments on Wednesday the 9th, and to vote on the bill as amended on Thursday the 10th. The authorization bill not only contained $2.13 billion for 1973 for foreign military assistance and refugee relief, but it also included Section 13, a committee amendment, which was the Foreign Affairs Committee's response to the O'Neill caucus directive.[156]

After the announcement, discussion of Section 13 ensued. The original Morgan-Hamilton provision called for the termination of U.S. sea and air operations over Indochina and the withdrawal of all U.S. forces "not later than October 1, 1972." It was subject to three conditions:

1. a cease-fire between U.S. and North Vietnam to the extent necessary to achieve safe withdrawal of the remaining U.S. forces,
2. release of all American prisoners of war held by North Vietnam and Viet Cong, and
3. accounting of all Americans missing in action.[157]

At the whip coffee, Representative Clem Zablocki informed his fellow colleagues, the zone whips, that all the main arguments concerning the Morgan-Hamilton committee amendment, Section 13, were presented clearly and succinctly in the committee report. The proponents of the measure recommended a retention of the Morgan-Hamilton provision on the following grounds:

1. It advised the President of acceptable and essential conditions of withdrawal, while leaving him the responsibility and the flexibility to negotiate an end to U.S. involvement.
2. It set realistic and achievable conditions of withdrawal by providing for a U.S.-North Vietnam cease-fire rather than what Hamilton called the "Administration's impractical general cease-fire

through Indochina," which had been repeatedly rejected by the other side.

3. It recognized that true American interest in Indochina would lower the level of violence in that area of the world and would encourage the political forces in the area to come to a mutually acceptable accommodation.[158]

In the opinion of those committee members who supported the amendment, "Section 13 is thoroughly consistent with Vietnamization and it is a natural and logical extension of it."[159]

Naturally, however, the Administration opposed the committee amendment, and its position was clearly presented in the supplemental views of the report, paralleling the arguments Clem Zablocki had given for supporting the Buchanan substitute on June 13. Opponents opined in the committee's report that the Morgan-Hamilton provision would not secure American prisoner release because "it does not meet Hanoi's principal demand that we overthrow President Thieu and cease all aid to the government of South Vietnam. It would upset delicate negotiations and would adversely affect the situation on the battlefield in South Vietnam, because it seeks simply to end U.S. participation in the conflict."[160]

Most importantly, by setting a date only two months away, the United States would be making a promise it could not conceivably keep. "Suppose, for instance," argued the Republican members of the Foreign Affairs Committee, "that Hanoi agreed to American conditions late in September. How could we withdraw all our troops within a month?"[161]

Two additional views in opposition to the Morgan-Hamilton provision were expressed by members of the Foreign Affairs Committee in the committee report. Republican Representative Paul Findley (Illinois) argued his opposition because it would not permit the President to settle the war by offering North Vietnam a better deal than that provided for in the Section 13 provision. In other words, Findley believed it seriously limited Nixon's flexibilities in the negotiations. In his opinion, the amendment stated only minimum terms for withdrawal.

"If an expression of Congressional policy is deemed necessary, it should be more carefully drafted," Findley said.[162]

Moreover, Republican Representative Vander Jagt (Michigan) opposed the Morgan-Hamilton provision on grounds that such expressions should be by separate resolution: H.J.Res. 1225, the Buchanan substitute, passed in June, was the "proper vehicle for House consideration of this issue rather than an amendment to the security assistance legislation which may well be defeated with the inclusion of such an amendment."[163] Knowing that the Buchanan resolution would most likely not reach the President's desk, perhaps he was suggesting that a simple or concurrent resolution expressing the sense of Congress did not legally bind the President's hands as an amendment to the foreign aid bill or a joint resolution would.

These arguments, contained so concisely in the committee report, would provide the main focus for the projected House floor debate on Section 13.

Following the announcement at the whip coffee of the date for House floor consideration of the foreign aid bill, the apparatus for seeking approval of the Morgan-Hamilton-Whalen amendment was set in motion. Before he adjourned the whip meeting, O'Neill reminded the zone whips that Section 13 was the legislative response to the caucus action of April 20.

O'Neill was especially pleased by the committee action and was confident of success. To get Chairman Morgan and the majority of the Foreign Affairs Committee, longtime supporters of Administration policy in Vietnam, to endorse an end-the-war amendment was more than encouraging. This was the first time a House committee had ever sent such a proposal to the floor.

O'Neill firmly believed that after years of taking the antiwar votes merely as procedural motions on Senate bills, the House would obtain its rightful and long-overdue opportunity to confront the withdrawal issue head-on.

***

The day before general debate began on the foreign aid measure—Monday, August 7—O'Neill, as majority whip and as the author of the Democratic caucus resolution that had given impetus to this committee amendment, Section 13 of the foreign aid legislation, sent a letter. It was drafted jointly in a meeting among his legislative assistant and Fred and Dave of Common Cause and sent to all Democratic members, reminding them (as he had the zone whips) that the withdrawal provision in the foreign aid bill was in response to the caucus action supported by 144 Democrats.[164]

The legislative assistant worked closely once again with Fred and Dave, as she had in the days prior to the caucus, taking an attendance check of DSG members. They learned that attendance would be nearly 100 percent for Thursday, the day of the vote on Section 13.

In addition to the "Dear Colleague" letter to members, O'Neill offered assistance to Chairman Morgan and to Lee Hamilton, who asked that he speak out vigorously on behalf of the committee amendment on the House floor, since the fight would come on an attempt to strike the Morgan-Hamilton provision from the bill. O'Neill gave them his commitment to speak on the committee amendment. But there was really nothing more he could do. The responsibility for floor-managing the bill rested with Chairman Morgan and the members of the Foreign Affairs Committee, including Whalen, who would offer his own amendment to change the date.

While Speaker Albert's and Majority Leader Boggs's positions were crucial, both had refused to say publicly how they would vote. John Gardner, chairman of Common Cause, strongly criticized Speaker Albert for his silence. "His failure to speak out in support of the amendment could well spell the difference between victory and defeat. The issues are too important . . . to maintain a condition of perpetual indecision."[165]

On Monday, after O'Neill had finished composing his letter to Democratic colleagues, he paid a visit to the Speaker and Majority Leader. Both tacitly assured him that they would endorse the Chairman's position to extend the date to December 31. Yet they would not comment on how they would vote if Whalen's amendment failed and a Democratic or Republican attempt were made to strike Section 13 of the foreign aid bill.[166] Because there was no unambiguous leadership position, no whip count had been taken on the Morgan-Hamilton amendment, known as Section 13. Of course, no whip count would have been ordered on Whalen's amendment since it was offered by a minority member.

While the position of the two top Democratic leaders was unclear, the President's position was quite lucid. He called the language of Section 13 to the foreign aid bill "totally unacceptable." It did not include his requirement for a universal cease-fire in Indochina, rather than just a cease-fire between the United States and North Vietnam, and "it merely called for arrangements for release of prisoners without requiring an actual release prior to U.S. pullout." The Administration argued that any proposal setting a deadline without major conditions "would encourage Hanoi to refuse to negotiate seriously for a peace settlement in the hope that Congress would simply force the United States to pull out."[167]

To leave no doubts on the Administration's firm and unyielding position on Section 13, chief White House lobbyist Dick Cook made the rounds to Republican and Southern Democratic members of the House on Monday and Tuesday. Interviewed by *The Washington Post* on Monday afternoon, Dick Cook predicted that the withdrawal provision would be rejected by twenty votes.

Meanwhile, backers of the Section 13 provision were claiming, in another interview, that the committee amendment would receive more than 200 votes. Both sides seemed confident of success, and until the hour of the vote, the outcome was uncertain. Neither side seemed to pay any attention to the potentially troublesome Whalen amendment.

Lay It on the Table

CHAPTER 14

The House Casts a Vote: The Tragic Flaw of Committee Indecision

Thus conscience doth make cowards of us all,
And thus the native hue of resolution
Is sicklied o'er with the pale cast of thought,
And enterprises of great pith and moment
With this regard their currents turn awry
And lose the name of action.

—from Shakespeare's *Hamlet* (Act 3, Scene 1)

The Majority Leader scheduled three days for House floor consideration of the Foreign Assistance Act of 1972: on Tuesday, general debate; on Wednesday, reading for amendments under the five-minute rule (a House rule that allows each member five minutes to speak); and on Thursday, concluding consideration.

Because Section 13 was the next-to-last section of the thirty-page bill, the House did not reach that provision for debate until Thursday afternoon.

It was not until then, when Whalen rose to offer his amendment to Section 13, that the tragic flaw of an October deadline was fully realized. The debate that ensued was a strident, polarizing clash over the consequences of changing that date to December. Whalen's amendment, which was meant to offer a more realistic deadline and give it bipartisan support, became a rallying point for both Democrats and Republicans to attack. Regrettably, the dispute overshadowed the main goal of the House going on record with an amendment to terminate American involvement in Vietnam.

Spearheading the opposition to the Whalen amendment were the House Minority Leader Gerald Ford (Michigan) and Wayne Hays (Ohio), both of whom supported the Administration's Vietnamization policy. In their House floor remarks, they charged forcefully that the Whalen amendment to Section 13 of the Foreign Assistance Act would extend the war and killing for ninety more days. These remarks were well calculated with the specific intent to split the war critics in half.

As Minority Leader Ford pointed out, "When they want to extend the war ninety more days, all their credibility in my opinion goes down the drain. The President is daily seeking to end the war by negotiations. I do not think an October 1 [or] a December 31 date will help that effort in any way whatsoever. This amendment will add to the tragedies and casualties in Vietnam."[168]

Hays argued that Whalen's amendment "gives us some idea of the ridiculousness of this whole situation. In committee, Whalen had supported the amendment to get the war over by October, [and] part of the argument was to keep it out of the election campaign. Now he wants to draw it on right through the election campaign."[169]

In other words, Ford and Hays were accusing any liberal who voted for the Whalen amendment of voting to extend the war and the killing for ninety more days. Any dove who was willing to compromise on the date to get an end-the-war provision passed by the House would be in a no-win situation akin to political suicide.

"There are two separate amendments—the original . . . amendment which has a cutoff of October 1 . . . [and this,] another Whalen amendment to extend the war by congressional sanction until the 31st of December."[170] Wayne Hays was unkindly and wrongfully placing the blame on Whalen for three additional months of war.

Abzug summed up the feelings of the ultra-liberals—like Drinan, Rosenthal, and Dellums—when she stated, "I am willing to accept October 1. I am not willing to accept December 31, and the reason I am not willing to accept December 31 is because we are killing. . . . So, Mr. Chairman, I ask the members to defeat the amendment to extend the date to December 31. Let us stop this killing."[171]

Ready to challenge Abzug, his perennial rival, Chairman Morgan rose to counter the argument that a vote for the December deadline was a vote to extend the killing. Instead, he argued that it was a compromise to give the end-the-war amendment a reasonable chance for passage. He pointed out that, pragmatically and realistically, the date of October 1 was impossible: "The Senate will not complete action on this legislation in the three remaining weeks after we return on September 5. Anybody who is interested in a realistic date will support the amendment of the gentleman from Ohio."[172]

And with that, the debate was ended. The vote was taken on the amendment offered by "the gentleman from Ohio," Mr. Whalen. The results: 109 yeas and 304 nays.[173] The Whalen amendment was rejected.

Democrats on the Foreign Affairs Committee who opposed the Whalen amendment were Dellums, Diggs, Fountain, Hays, and Rosenthal. The Democratic leadership, including Speaker Albert, Majority Leader Boggs, Majority Whip O'Neill, and Chairman Morgan, all voted in the minority in support of the Whalen amendment. Other Democrats voting against the amendment were the leading ultra-liberal war doves like Father Drinan, the original sponsor of the 1972 peace bill; Bella Abzug and the rest of the liberal New York delegation; the members of the Congressional Black Caucus; and a majority of the New England delegation. All of these Democratic doves who voted against Whalen were vigorous supporters of antiwar amendments and the O'Neill caucus resolution; yet they voted against the Whalen amendment because they refused to go on record to extend the war ninety days.

In politics, perception is reality. These doves refused to be perceived as supporters of extending the war, *even if that extension was the means to end the war.* Concerned only with optics,[174] the antiwar liberals were unwilling to compromise.

Perhaps Section 13, perfected by the Whalen amendment in the Foreign Affairs Committee rather than as an amendment on the House floor, could have been accepted by the majority of the House members. Why? Because for the first time in the history of the House antiwar movements it had the endorsement of the top Democratic leadership as well as support from a majority of members of the House Foreign Affairs Committee.

But the hawks had done their homework well. They knew that by framing the debate in a way that pierced the heart of the dove argument, they put many uncompromising liberal doves in an untenable position: that a vote for the Whalen amendment was a vote to prolong the war. The war could have been over by the end of the year. But intent on getting their way or no way at all, the antiwar liberals, by their refusal to compromise, ensured the war would drag on, body counts would increase, and antiwar protests would become more violent.

In the beginning of this book, O'Neill struggled with a Hamlet-like dilemma ("To be, or not to be"): Should he take the lead at the Democratic caucus and set in motion the criteria for the House to end the war? It was a tough decision with certain consequences either way he chose. But that is where his comparison to the Danish prince ends. O'Neill considered his choices, weighed the consequences, consulted his moral compass, and *acted*. He followed up and followed through.

Hamlet, on the other hand, over-analyzed his choices, and his indecision led to inaction, which led to his demise. Similarly, the members of the Foreign Affairs Committee debated and dragged their feet, and their stalling led to the tragic flaw of the resolution—the impossible deadline. O'Neill had taken the role of change agent by introducing a resolution to rally the Democrats to end the war. However, he had no control over the committee, to which he had to hand over the reins. When the House Foreign Affairs Committee failed to do its due diligence, it shattered the opportunity O'Neill provided.

Like the Foreign Affairs Committee, Hamlet's flaw was this inability to act resolutely in his best interest, as well as that of his family and country. Perhaps the same can be said about the liberal doves. Their big, bleeding hearts—although well meaning—got in the way of their work, and they were unable to focus on what was best for the United States. The argument shifted from realistically ending the war by the end of the year to extending "the killing" by three months, the latter of which they could not stomach. Missing the forest to critique the trees, their conflict led to confusion, which led to the demise of the end-of-war legislation.

***

After the House defeated the Whalen amendment, Richard Bolling (Missouri), a top-ranking Democrat on the powerful Rules Committee, next offered an amendment to strike out Section 13. As a supporter of the traditional deference to the President in decisions of war and peace, he believed the Section 13 withdrawal provision attempted to put limitations on the President's ability to end the war. This condition he could not accept. "Only the President can negotiate an end to this war under the Constitution, so the provision would be meaningless," he stated on the House floor.[175]

Hale Boggs, the majority leader, rising to speak on behalf of the Bolling amendment, put the whole debate into its proper perspective. He pointed out why he voted for the Whalen amendment, seeking meaningful legislation to end the war. It was an extemporaneous oration that must rank among the finest speeches Boggs ever articulated on the House floor. Little did House members realize that this would be one of the last times they would hear their Majority Leader speak on legislation:

> "As a legislative body we must always consider whether what we are doing is simply an empty and useless expression, or whether there is some genuine hope of realizing our objective. . . .
>
> "There is no chance whatsoever of this section, as now constituted, ever becoming law. . . . There is not time for this bill to reach the Executive before October 1.
>
> "I voted, along with the Speaker, a moment ago, for the December 31 cutoff date with the other language in Section 13. I voted that way because the members of my Democratic caucus voted . . . as I did, for legislation intended to end U.S.

involvement in Vietnam. . . . I had every intention today of voting for this provision with a December 31 cutoff date, and I would have voted for it.

"But I am not going to stand here now to do some thing, which I consider a vain and useless thing and which could be misinterpreted all over the world.

"I believe the thing for us to do now is to support the motion before us."

The Majority Leader stated further:

"It would be a poor reflection upon the judgment of the House of Representatives for us to enact an ineffectual provision today.

"So here we are this afternoon about to vote on a provision, which cannot possibly become law even if passed today. I say with all due deference and with all respect for my colleagues that I am as dedicated to world peace and to the end of U.S. involvement in Vietnam as any man in this body.

"But, as one to whom you have trusted some degree of leadership, I cannot in good conscience do anything other than to support the gentleman from Missouri [Mr. Bolling]."[176]

When the Majority Leader finished, he received a long round of applause from both sides of the aisle.

While the House floor debate droned on, the arguments continued along the pros and cons of an appropriate withdrawal deadline. These arguments had been rehashed and reiterated on numerous occasions before; they obfuscated the real issue of the congressional role to end the war.

Standing in the back of the House chamber, having heard Hale Boggs's fine oration, O'Neill and his legislative assistant knew the die had been cast by the remarks of the distinguished Majority Leader. The Whip realized that his leader had convinced enough members with his rational and reasonable logic that if the House voted for the October 1 deadline this late in the legislative year, it would be an empty gesture. No doubt existed after Boggs finished speaking that the Bolling amendment to strike Section 13 would be adopted.

However, O'Neill, though understanding it was an exercise in futility, felt bound by his commitment to Doc Morgan and Lee Hamilton to participate in the debate. Unlike Hamlet, he knew how to make crucial decisions in moments of crisis, and this debate was one of those moments.

He had built multiple bridges of friendship in the House over the years to earn the trust and respect of members on both sides of the aisle. Through his April caucus resolution, O'Neill had given a real tiger-like impetus to an end-the-war proposal by building a consensus, offering a compromise that was acceptable and winnable in caucus, and engaging in teamwork with other House members. He now felt obligated to address the House on the striking of Section 13.

Inspired by the responsibility he felt as a legislative leader and compelled by the strength of his moral convictions, O'Neill walked down the aisle to the front of the chamber to seek recognition from the presiding officer. Once recognized, the Majority Whip began:

"Mr. Chairman, I would be remiss as a member of Congress if I did not take the floor today to speak against this amendment, in view of the fact that I have been in this well so many times in the last five years in opposition to this war.

"I heard our great majority leader get up here today—and I have the greatest respect for him, and I know he was speaking as an individual—to tell us how he felt on this amendment and explain the technicality of the amendment.

"For eighteen years I have sat in the Committee on Rules next to the gentleman from Missouri [Mr. Bolling]. There is nobody in this Congress for whom I have more respect, for his knowledge, ability, vision, and the courage he always portrays. But the amendment as offered by [Bolling] is stating that Congress has no role in determining American foreign policy. The Constitution says that Congress has the right to declare war.

"This amendment makes clear that Congress has no right, has no stake in ending the war in Indochina.

"But I say this: *If Congress does have a role in declaring a war, it does have a role in ending the war.*

"Do we play a part in foreign policy?

"We helped the Administration administer a policy because we told them what the true feeling of the American public was.

"There is no question in my mind that those of us in the minority—and I can read this Congress, it is one of my duties as majority whip to be able to read this Congress—will not prevail. I do not expect that the Bolling amendment can be defeated today.

"Do we set foreign policy? No, we do not set foreign policy. But we are the voice of the grassroots, the voice of the people of America, and the people of America are fed up with this war. They want us to spend the money on the priorities that will get America rolling again. That is what this is all about.

"I admire the courage of all those who speak on either side of this issue today. The colloquy is good for the American public.

"The Morgan-Hamilton provision, regardless of what may possibly happen and though it may never be enacted into law, I believe is an expression of how the American people feel about this war."[177] Alexander Hamilton would have agreed with him—the House reflects the sentiment of America!

In his speech, O'Neill expressed his personal conviction, not only about the Vietnam War and those convictions of a majority of the American people but also about the rightful role of Congress in declaring and ending an unpopular war.

Alas, all time for debate had expired.

"The question is on the amendment offered by the gentleman from Missouri," said the presiding officer.

On a recorded teller vote, there were 228 ayes, 178 nays, and 27 not voting.[178] The Bolling amendment to strike Section 13 was adopted.

The largest vote that the House had ever cast in support of a withdrawal deadline had been in 1971, for the second Mansfield amendment (with a six-month termination date)—193 votes, or 25 short of a majority. The 178 votes cast for Section 13, fixing a withdrawal date, fell 15 short of that previous high.

The controversy over the October 1 versus December 31 deadline provided a face-saving opportunity for some fence-sitters to vote against the provision as useless, impractical, and unrealistic. It fuzzed over the O'Neill caucus directive of an end-the-war amendment that had been steered through the standard legislative process in the House. Furthermore, it relegated to the back burner what the Majority Whip saw as the real issue of the debate—that if Congress had a role in declaring a war, then it had a role in ending it. As the voice of the American people, it had a role in determining American foreign policy; the constitutional power of the purse gave Congress a "role in spending the money on the priorities that would get America rolling again."[179]

Section 13 of the 1972 foreign aid legislation was the first time a House committee had ever sent to the House floor a proposal with a date certain to end the Vietnam War.

Undeniably, the tragic mistake surrounding the date had been made in the full committee markup. The committee members, when drafting Section 13, adopted the old Morgan-Hamilton provision promulgated by the Democratic members of the committee on May 10, neglecting to change the date to a more practical one. Given the delay of the Foreign Affairs Committee in response to the O'Neill caucus directive, the members of the committee could have easily provided a more realistic date of December 31 during markup of the foreign aid bill—rather than during the last minutes of debate on the House floor via the Whalen amendment. This decision to offer a workable date should have been advanced by Chairman Morgan, whose respect from committee members most likely would have garnered the support of the language of the Whalen amendment during committee deliberation.

Justifiably, O'Neill had never been sure where Morgan's allegiances lay. The Ole Doc was unassuming—vocally supportive and encouraging to O'Neill's face, yet his subtle actions—or inactions—may have been telling a different story. He, like Hamlet, had hesitated on the caucus directive. But was it contrived or typical congressional delay?

After the vote on the Bolling amendment, one member of the New England delegation exclaimed to O'Neill's legislative assistant, "Doc Morgan knew this would happen all along. He never really changed his position on the war."[180]

Had the House Foreign Affairs Chairman intentionally neglected to change the date in markup? Had he surmised correctly that the leading war critics would have a falling out over the deadline? Since the votes in committee prevailed in favor of the doves' position to end the war, the hawks' only hope of defeating an end-the-war provision on the House floor was to cloud the issue of terminating American involvement in Indochina with a polemic over the date.

Chairman Morgan was highly offended at such a suggestion. All members of the Foreign Affairs Committee vouched for the sincere motivation of their chairman in trying to report out a provision that clearly followed the directive of the O'Neill caucus resolution.[181] The committee was so anxious to report out the foreign aid bill as quickly as possible that it simply forgot to change the date. (Yet, would it have been so anxious if it hadn't dawdled on the issue for a whole month?)

In reality, then, the House did not have a clear vote on the Vietnam amendment on August 10, 1972. Was the outcome inevitable? Yes; with the dispute over the date, Section 13, the Morgan-Hamilton provision, was doomed to failure. But would the outcome have been different if the change of date had been made in committee?

Unquestionably, O'Neill believed "15 to 20 more votes" would have been in support of Section 13 with the language of the Morgan-Hamilton-Whalen provision adopted during committee markup. Therefore, the vote on August 10 would most likely have been greater than the previous high of 193.[182] The vote might have been as high as 198 or 200, still short of the 218 minimum votes required in the House to beat the Bolling motion to strike Section 13 with a December 31st deadline. Moreover, O'Neill mused that the House floor debate would have focused on the issue of Congress's role to end the war rather than a fight over which date to stop the killing.

Would the Morgan-Hamilton-Whalen provision drafted in committee have prevailed on the House floor? In analyzing the mood of the House, O'Neill says no: "The time had not yet come for the House to approve a congressional initiative to set a date certain for termination of American involvement in Indochina."[183]

And so, with the defeat of Section 13 of the Foreign Assistance Act, the Morgan-Hamilton provision, it seemed the House of Representatives was no closer in 1972 to the passage of an amendment to end the Vietnam War than it was in 1971. But that regrettable scenario elicits merely the disparaging part of this story.

The whole purpose of the O'Neill-Gibbons caucus resolution, which directed the Democrats on the Foreign Affairs Committee to report legislation within thirty days, was clear. It enabled the House of Representatives to work its will for the first time on the Vietnam issue through the standard legislative process. Although the final House floor vote was not the result O'Neill wanted, he could only feel some satisfaction in his assiduous leadership and management of the majority party to assure the People's House voted on a date certain to end the war. This much, at least, had been accomplished on August 10, 1972, when the members of the House of Representatives voted to strike the Morgan-Hamilton provision (Section 13) from the Foreign Assistance Act of 1972. O'Neill had accomplished a legislative milestone to empower the House to reach this point. The effort was not wasted.

CHAPTER 15

The End of the War and the Beginning of a New House

The risk of asserting himself in ending the Vietnam War might have jeopardized O'Neill's position as whip or altered his climb up the House leadership ladder. But he took the risk resolutely and without reservation because he believed it was the right course of action. If he lost any sleep over his decision, an impending tragedy would soon prove that the risk was not only worth taking, but it also put him in a better position to advance than before. He had no way of knowing that within two months after the House voted to strike Section 13, unforeseen disaster would hit. Its consequences would propel O'Neill into a position for which he was ready and forearmed.

The House floor vote on the Morgan-Hamilton amendment occurred August 10, 1972. Two months later, after a marathon thirty-plus-hour session, the House adjourned for the year. It was a presidential election year, and all 435 House members were up for reelection—unless they had decided not to run again. Those who sought reelection were ready to return home to their constituent districts to campaign.

Following the House adjournment, Hale Boggs immediately took off to campaign in Alaska for Representative Nicolas "Nick" Begich. As majority leader, he often campaigned for Democratic members in their districts, and Nick Begich was facing tough opposition for reelection to the House. On the flight from Juneau to Anchorage, the small Cessna plane piloted by an Alaskan bush pilot disappeared. All passengers, including Boggs and Begich, disappeared with the plane on October 16, 1972. Their bodies were never found.

The House members, shocked and in disbelief at the tragic loss of their majority leader, rallied around O'Neill, next in line to fill the now-vacant position. Boggs's wife, Corinne "Lindy" Boggs, decided to run for her husband's House seat in their Louisiana district with O'Neill's encouragement. But she was no political rookie. Mrs. Boggs had managed her husband's campaign, as well as many others, and she had chaired the inaugural ball committees for Kennedy and Johnson. Active among the wives of the congressmen, she was well liked and accepted by all members of Congress. Lindy Boggs—shrewd, resilient, and brimming with Southern charm and social graces—was what her husband would have called "a real lady," who seemed to always get what she wanted. Moreover, everyone was happy to give it to her!

She endorsed O'Neill to take her late husband's place as majority leader, as did Boggs's staff. O'Neill consulted with Speaker Albert, who also strongly supported him in this role. So, at the appropriate time, and with the Boggs family's blessing, O'Neill let the Democratic members know he would be a candidate in the caucus for majority leader.

The House presumed their majority leader dead on January 3, 1973, with H.Res. 1 of the 93rd Congress, which declared a vacancy left by Hale Boggs.[184] O'Neill had no opposition and was elected the House majority leader.

As majority whip, O'Neill had just led the big fight to end the Vietnam War. It was an important dimension for him; it ingratiated him with the liberal caucus, the Democratic Study Group. It showed that he was willing to fight for his principles and for some of the liberal causes they championed. They saw him as a real leader who had built strong relationships in the House. He knew how to work the House and its members, and he knew how to ask for and count votes when needed. The issue-oriented liberals supported him as leader, but so did the party regulars. Even the Southern conservatives liked O'Neill, despite their differences in political philosophy and their support for the President in the conduct of the war. They trusted and respected him as a man who kept his word.

***

During O'Neill's transition from majority whip to majority leader, American combat support in Vietnam was withdrawn. President Nixon signed the Paris Peace Accords, ending U.S. involvement in the war, on January 27, 1973. The civil war continued for two more years despite the communists' speedy gains. Without U.S. combat support, South Vietnamese forces could not withstand the North Vietnamese advance.

Saigon, South Vietnam's capital, fell in 1975. An unforgettable "Saigon Moment"[185] was forever etched indelibly in the American psyche: images of American helicopters idling on the rooftop of the U.S. embassy in Saigon as the North Vietnamese entered the city; frantic Americans scrambling for a spot in one of the helicopters landed on the roof to quickly airlift the civilians before the North Vietnamese soldiers arrived to cut them off. It was a frightening, chaotic, and massive undertaking, fraught with missteps and *danger*. Yet neither Democrats nor Republicans blamed Gerald Ford, the current commander in chief, for the execution of the evacuation. Communist North Vietnam took over the entire country. This after decades of fighting and millions of lives lost.

The United States had entered and sustained its involvement in the Vietnam War for three major reasons: (1) to prevent the spread of communism after WWII, citing the Domino Theory—if Vietnam fell to communists, all Southeast Asia would be lost to communism; (2) to use the Gulf of Tonkin incident as provocation for direct U.S. combat involvement in a civil war; (3) to find an "honorable peace" through Vietnamization rather than a precipitous withdrawal, thus keeping American troops in Vietnam.

After suffering a terrible defeat in 1954, the French colonial power dominating Vietnam negotiated an end to its involvement, establishing a communist government in North Vietnam and a democratic government in South Vietnam. Once the French left, a power vacuum existed; the U.S. supported South Vietnam with military and political advisers throughout the 1950s and early 1960s to contain communism in Southeast Asia. Following the Gulf of Tonkin incident in 1964, President Johnson escalated U.S. military involvement beyond that of advisers to direct combat with the North Vietnamese and Viet Cong. The 1968 Tet Offensive attacks by the communist forces in Vietnam resulted in heavy losses for the U.S. and South Vietnamese and became a defining moment for public opinion about the war.[186]

Increasing protests at home, dwindling public support for U.S. involvement, and the inability to win the war by the late 1960s ended Johnson's presidency in 1968. After 1969, President Nixon began to reduce the level of U.S. combat troops in Vietnam, yet the policy remained to achieve an "honorable peace." In 1970, Nixon expanded the war when U.S. ground troops entered Cambodia for the purpose of destroying the communist supply lines for military operations against South Vietnam. Still the North Vietnamese and the Viet Cong could not be stopped, and Nixon's Vietnamization policy, absent action by Congress to terminate the war, dragged on until the Paris Peace Accords in January 1973.

At about the same time, the Senate revived the Case-Church amendment to the foreign aid bill of 1972, which had previously been defeated. This was the amendment that killed the Foreign Assistance Act that year and had attempted to end American military action in Cambodia, Laos, and Vietnam by cutting off monetary support. The new cutoff date was August 15, 1973, and it prohibited any further military involvement in the conflict.[187] It passed in the House and the Senate with numbers greater than the two-thirds majority needed to override a presidential veto. In the meantime, the draft was called off, the remaining troops were withdrawn, and 591 POWs came home.[188]

During O'Neill's tenure as majority leader, the passage of the War Powers Act (WPA) on November 7, 1973, over President Nixon's veto was Congress's most immediate reaction to the end of the Vietnam War. It was, in essence, a shortsighted attempt to reassert congressional power as a coequal branch in the war-making decisions—resulting, in part, from the "informed acquiescence" of the Gulf of Tonkin Resolution. Its policy purpose was to prevent another Vietnam situation that was initiated and pursued solely by presidential action. More so, it attempted to place restraint or supervision over President Nixon's abuses of power, which reflected the political environment at this specific time in U.S. history.

The act had unintended consequences for all future presidents.

The House had failed to terminate the Vietnam War through the directive of the O'Neill caucus resolution. The Senate had also failed, time and time again, to exercise its constitutional power of the purse to cut off funding for the Vietnam War until the Case-Church amendment was finally adopted in 1973. The War Powers Act threw out the traditional bipartisan cooperation in foreign policy, where "politics stops at the water's edge"; instead, it provided a questionable constitutional dividing line between congressional power to declare war and presidential power as commander in chief.

After the United States' secret bombing and incursion into Cambodia in May 1970, it took three years of extensive hearings by Zablocki's House Foreign Affairs subcommittee to develop the War Powers Act. The Senate, meanwhile, was developing its own version through its Foreign Relations Committee. In 1973, the House and Senate enacted a War Powers Act, H.J.Res. 542, by adopting in a conference compromise much of the House bill.[189] Clearly, the House had altered its position on matters of war and peace. The measure of how far the House had changed reflected the O'Neill caucus directive, increased unpopularity of the Vietnam War, the Watergate scandal enveloping the White House, and elections in 1972, which changed the composition of House members.

The new law created procedures and timetables for presidential reporting as well as a process of consultation between the executive and legislative branches involving the commission of American troops in foreign combat missions. It is complex: Before U.S. troops are introduced "into hostilities or . . . situations where imminent involvement in hostilities" may occur, the President must consult with Congress "in every possible instance." If troops are committed into hostilities, absent a declaration of war, the President must submit a report to Congress within forty-eight hours. The President must terminate involvement of troops within sixty to ninety days thereafter, "unless Congress has taken affirmative action to approve the troop deployment by passing a concurrent resolution."[190]

President Nixon vetoed the WPA because it limited presidential power as commander in chief. Clem Zablocki, who had opposed Majority Whip O'Neill's caucus directive and felt unbound by it during Foreign Affairs Committee deliberation, asked Majority Leader O'Neill to help on the veto override with DSG members who had voted against the war powers bill, believing it gave too much power to the President. O'Neill complied with Zablocki's request, working on the liberals, including Bella Abzug, who switched her opposition to the bill to vote for the override.[191] The House overrode the veto by four votes one week after the "Saturday Night Massacre."[192]

O'Neill opined that "Congress had to enact the War Powers Act in order to control [Nixon]."[193]

Since its passage, the WPA has had its share of supporters and detractors. Proponents argue the law is necessary to check presidential ability to deploy American troops in hostilities abroad and to sustain those efforts without congressional approval. Opponents argue that (1) the act failed to create better cooperation between the executive branch and Congress in war-making decisions;

(2) it is too restrictive and inflexible on presidential ability to respond to foreign threats; (3) it gives the President free reign to commit American forces into hostilities for up to ninety days; and (4) a congressional concurrent resolution cannot constitutionally bind a president. It can only express the sense or wisdom of both chambers, House and Senate. It has no force of law since it defies the Presentment Clause of the Constitution.[194]

Today, Congress is grappling with whether to repeal or to continue authorizations for use of military force (AUMF) under the WPA. In addition, Congress has introduced the Reclamation of War Powers Act in 2021. The House measure has two main provisions:

1. Congress will fund the introduction of U.S. armed forces into hostilities only with a declaration of war, specific statutory authorization, or a national emergency created by an attack or imminent threat of attack upon the United States, its territories or possessions, or the Armed Forces.
2. Presidents requesting a declaration of war or Authorization for Use of Military Force (AUMF) must issue a report outlining the threat faced, the objectives and justifications of the conflict, and a description of the anticipated scope and duration of the action.[195]

The Senate measure would

1. define *hostilities* as any operation involving the use of force expanding the current defini-

tion of the WPA, which applies only to combat troops on the ground;

2. shorten presidential ability to engage in those hostilities from sixty to twenty days and automatically terminate funding for an operation if a president fails to secure congressional support for the venture by that deadline.[196]

These proposed acts are works in progress; they continue the same arguments of proponents and opponents, pitting the Congress's power to declare war under Article I of the Constitution against the President's authority as commander in chief under Article II of the Constitution. Enactment of the Reclamation of War Powers Act into law is highly unlikely in this current Congress.

Despite paying lip service to the WPA, presidents have generally ignored the law. They have failed to send reports to Congress under the WPA's timetables, and the sixty-to-ninety-day provision has never been used to end military operations abroad. Furthermore, the interpretation of the term *consult* differs between President and Congress. Presidents see it as the Commander in Chief's sole decision to deploy American troops into hostilities abroad. To consult with Congress means that they inform Congress *after* making the decision to deploy. Congress, on the other hand, sees itself as a coequal branch in matters of war and peace—an integral part of the decision-making process. To consult means that the President meets with Congress *before* making a decision. In fact, the idea is to make the decision together. This rarely, if ever, happens.

**

The ending of the Vietnam War and the passage of the War Powers Act occurred early in O'Neill's tenure as majority leader. Under his watch, he actively encouraged changes in the House. Early in the 93rd Congress, he supported the freshmen's special order on "impoundment," an issue that was quickly gaining momentum.

The process of appropriation is this: Congress appropriates funds by passing a bill. The President signs or vetoes the appropriation bill. Congress overrides or sustains it. When Congress appropriates and the President signs the bill into law, the President is mandated by the Constitution to spend the appropriation. And yet presidents since Franklin Delano Roosevelt, and even before, impounded some monies. Usually, it was an emergency, in which a legitimate reason existed for the President to hold up and not spend the money that had been appropriated. However, Nixon abused impoundment to the point where it became a constitutional crisis over which branch, legislative or executive, holds the "power of the purse."

Nixon expected the Congress to appropriate his agenda. If Congress initiated programs he opposed, he refused to spend the money. He was setting his policy agenda by impounding money. Calling his impoundment policy the "imperial presidency,"[197] Congress passed the Budget and Impoundment Control Act (BICA) of 1974.

BICA controlled presidential impoundment with a new procedure called "rescissions and deferrals," set up Budget Committees in the House and Senate, and established the Congressional Budget Office, which became the arm of the Congress to obtain accurate information about the revenues, economy, and deficit consequences of budget decisions. It also set a timetable for budget action by the Congress, placed spending caps on the Appropriations Committee, and changed the fiscal year from July 1 to October 1.[198] The latter was a huge change. It reasserted Congress's constitutional authority as a coequal branch and that the "power of the purse" belonged to the legislative branch. Today, Congress fails to follow its timely mandates, although the BICA law is still in effect.

As majority leader, and later as speaker, O'Neill responded favorably to the changes in the composition of the House membership. The 93rd, 94th, and 95th Congresses (1973–1979) saw an increase in the Democratic majority, consisting of younger members elected to the House. For instance, seventy-six new Democrats were elected in 1974, the so-called "Watergate babies," and then forty-four more were elected in 1976.[199] These younger and newer members of the House had not run for office before and had not come up through the political system of serving in the state legislature before seeking election to Congress. They were proud and privileged to be members of Congress, and they had worked hard to win their elections.

However, the House did not experience simultaneously a great influx of women. For example, the number of women serving in the House grew merely from thirteen to twenty-one in the period between 1971 and 1981.[200] Yet newer male members elected in the same decade were less chauvinistic; they were much more respectful and accepting of women who had gone through the same process as they had to win their elections. These newer members never expressed the idea that "women don't belong here—this is our territory." Instead, they felt they were in it together—male and female members—because they were all change agents, working for the good of the people they represented.

Ella Grasso served in the House in the early seventies. She was sharp and dynamic, and when she entered a room, it glowed like a ray of sunshine. However, she expressed what most women who served at the time believed when she said to O'Neill's staff, "It would take me forever. I'll be dead and buried before I get into a position of power." She was very frustrated by the House as an institution—its tedium, the snail's pace by which women members could seek opportunity and rise to the top. So she decided to exit the House and run for governor of Connecticut. She ran and became the country's first woman elected governor in her own right (not succeeding her husband).[201]

As the 1970s progressed, the DSG grew in stature and began to look at other issues besides Vietnam. It sought to change the House to make it more open to opportunity for younger members by eliminating the automatic seniority system that determined committee chairs. Many of the new members—male and female—joined the Democratic Study Group to remove absolute control from the committee chairmen barons who were preventing them from achieving leadership positions on committees. It was positive change O'Neill accepted, welcomed, and embraced. Most importantly, with the support of the DSG and the newly elected, younger, more liberal members, Majority Leader O'Neill—and later Speaker O'Neill—democratized the House throughout the 1970s.

The democratization of the House was made possible by two changes. The first was the action by the Democratic caucus, which ratifies elections of committee chairmen, to vote down three committee chairmen. This unprecedented move broke the traditional seniority system. It sent a signal to all other committee chairmen that they now had to allow greater input from junior members on their respective committees. While the seniority system remained the norm for power in the House, it was no longer automatic, and chairmen no longer could exercise absolute control of their respective committees without potential consequences. The second change: assignment of members to committees was transferred from the Ways and Means to the Steering and Policy Committee, the executive board of the Democratic caucus.

Much of O'Neill's early years as majority leader (1973–1975) were consumed by the House impeachment investigation. New and veteran members alike were upset with the "imperial presidency." They wanted to see an investigation of the President, and O'Neill was to play a major role.

At first, Speaker Albert was cautious, concerned that it would look like a partisan vendetta—particularly because the House was fighting the President over impoundments. The impoundment issue had reached such a constitutional crisis, Republican members were chastising Majority Leader O'Neill and Speaker Albert, saying things like, "Oh, you just want to impeach, and you're going to use impoundment as an excuse to conduct an investigation."

Again, Tip O'Neill was decisive on this matter—one might even say clairvoyant. He had an uncanny sense that illegal conduct—nothing to do with impoundments—had occurred, and it emanated from the White House. He told House Judiciary Chairman Peter Rodino (New Jersey), "You better get ready to do this investigation."[202]

Like the Speaker, Pete Rodino was at first somewhat reluctant to move on impeachment. Yes, he was the chairman of the Judiciary Committee, which had jurisdiction over impeachments of public officials, including presidents. Yet Rodino was a little bit cautious because he was new on the job. His predecessor, Emanuel "Manny" Celler (New York), was a legendary legal scholar who had been chairman of the House Judiciary Committee for years. But then Elizabeth Holtzman, a political outsider, beat him in the 1972 election. It was incomprehensible that this unknown woman ousted Manny Celler! Nevertheless, she did, and Pete Rodino became the chairman of the Judiciary Committee—untried and new on the job.

Yet Tip O'Neill had every confidence in Pete Rodino. He knew him well and liked him. They came from the same type of background in urban politics. They had the same basic philosophy. He trusted Rodino to carry out the investigation in the right way. But he also realized that the House had to start this investigation at once—they had to determine whether or not President Nixon had obstructed justice and participated in a cover-up.

Majority Leader O'Neill kept importuning Carl Albert to draft the resolution to authorize the investigation. The House Judiciary Committee had been formed back in the early 1800s, and it was the committee members who floor managed the only other presidential impeachment: President Andrew Johnson after the Civil War. The precedent had been set over a hundred years before.

O'Neill's office researched the first presidential impeachment and the history of the House Judiciary Committee. The research found nothing that precluded the Judiciary Committee from conducting an impeachment investigation. O'Neill then spoke to Speaker Albert, who made the decision to launch the investigation. The House prepared a resolution (H.Res. 803)[203] authorizing the Judiciary Committee to investigate. And so the process began May 9, 1974.[204]

The term used constantly was "deliberate speed," as in, "The investigation shall be done with deliberate speed," which is an oxymoron. *Deliberate* means to deliberate over a period of time. But *speed* implies haste, which was not possible. The instruction was to do it right, to do it legally, and to make sure the Judiciary Committee was not engaged in any partisan vendetta. The Speaker and Majority Leader brought the Republicans on board to allow the investigation to begin by granting subpoena powers for the whole committee, not just the chairman and the ranking Republicans as was the norm.

On and on it went. The Judiciary Committee investigated and listened to all the tapes, which took weeks. As spun out as it was, it was a fascinating time to be in Washington, reading the daily *Washington Post* while sipping the first cup of coffee in the morning. Bob Woodward and Carl Bernstein reported on the scandal, and as the months dragged on, each article moved closer and closer to the President. Was there obstruction of justice in the White House? Did Nixon know about, participate in, or sanction the cover-up? Would these actions qualify as "high crimes and misdemeanors"?

During the weeks in which they listened to the tapes as part of the impeachment investigation, members of the Judiciary Committee had to enter the House chamber to vote. Usually, they would stay on the House floor for a while, chatting with other members before they returned to the tape-listening tedium. For many weeks, nothing emerged that seemed to be an impeachable offense. Still they met, and still they listened.

One day, O'Neill's legislative assistant was on the House floor during a vote. She noticed that the members of the Judiciary Committee came in, quickly voted, and disappeared. Then Chairman Rodino approached her and said, "Where's Tip? I've got to talk to him. Can you find him for me?"

"Yes, Mr. Chairman," she said, and swiftly walked to the Democratic Cloakroom to call Leo Diehl, the administrative assistant in the Leader's office.

"Find the Majority Leader and get him on the floor ASAP," she told him. "Something's happened in Judiciary, and its members are disappearing after they vote. Chairman Rodino has a very worried look on his face and wants to speak to the Majority Leader."[205]

A few minutes later, the Majority Leader appeared in the House chamber, and he and the Chairman talked. Rodino revealed to O'Neill the eighteen-minute gap in the tape recordings from the Nixon White House. O'Neill and Rodino knew then that the House had grounds for impeachment. The Judiciary Committee reported out three articles of impeachment on July 30, 1974. Nixon resigned the presidency on August 9, 1974.[206]

***

When Carl Albert retired at the end of 1976, Tip O'Neill was ready to succeed him. Like his majority leader predecessor, Hale Boggs, O'Neill was responsible for scheduling House floor legislation and frequently campaigned for Democratic House members. He expended a lot of time and energy, even on weekends, speaking at events and helping members seeking reelection in their districts. Campaigning helped O'Neill know the members better—to understand the politics and concerns of their districts. It was good preparation for the speakership. As majority leader, he could no longer serve as a member of any standing House committee, including the Rules Committee, where he had served for nearly twenty years. There was nowhere else to go but up. The next stop was Speaker of the House.

Lay It on the Table

CHAPTER 16

A New Era: The House Democratized

Once O'Neill became majority leader, the campaign was on to become speaker when Carl Albert retired. He benefited from the House democratization, which he spearheaded through his openness to new ideas and embracing change in how the House functioned. As the most popular man in the House, he had minimal opposition. Sam Gibbons ran against him, but O'Neill won handily. Again, he put Mrs. O'Brien's advice into action, asking for his colleagues' support. He took nothing for granted as a candidate for the speakership. He worked just as diligently as he had in the fight for the caucus resolution to the end the war.

At the start of the 95th Congress, Tip O'Neill was elected the forty-seventh Speaker of the U.S. House of Representatives. He served for ten years, a decade characterized by positive change to the House, just as was his mantra as majority whip and leader.

Speaker O'Neill shepherded the Steering and Policy Committee into real leadership strength. This committee was the Speaker's eyes and ears on processing bills through legislative committees, working with the chairmen to develop the Democratic policy agenda. Thus, the Speaker became more involved in the development of public policy on the committee level, which was a tremendous change.

One reform that aided democratization of the House going forward was taking away the assignment of members to committees from the Ways and Means Committee in late 1974 and early 1975.[207] This removed the assignment process away from special interests. Ways and Means has jurisdiction over Medicare, Medicaid, health insurance, taxes, social security—all very important matters. Every special interest goes before Ways and Means, and if it served as the committee to assign other House members to standing committees, lobbyists could have immense influence over which members were assigned to which committees—particularly lobbyists who had clients before those committees. This change was a noteworthy example of democratization of the House: more accountability, more transparency, and more disclosure.

Since the Steering and Policy Committee was the "committee on committees," which gave members of the majority party (Democrats) their assignments, it was divided into zones—similar yet different from the whip zones. Each zone's members elected one of their own to the Steering and Policy Committee, and that member would bargain back and forth with other committee members. Some wanted a specific, newly elected member from their zone to serve on such and such a committee. Others wanted their zone member on this or that committee, and they would negotiate. It was an open process.

With the defeat of automatic seniority to determine committee chairs, a change also occurred in subcommittee assignments. Each newly elected member was assigned to a full committee and then had his or her choice of which subcommittee he or she wanted. Before, the chairmen would assign each new member to a subcommittee, and that member had no choice in the matter.

This change helped women advance in the House, as they could choose the subcommittee on which they desired to serve rather than be assigned by the committee chairmen without their input. As they now had more opportunity to be assigned to the full committee of their choice, they could then choose a subcommittee to potentially build their seniority and eventually chair the full committee. This opened doors for women to attain positions of House leadership.

Today, women number 119 in the 117th Congress; the speaker is a woman; women chair seven committees, thirty-six subcommittees, and serve on all House committees, including the three most prestigious: Ways and Means, Rules, and Appropriations.[208] When O'Neill was majority whip, Edith Green (Pennsylvania) was the only subcommittee chairwoman, and no woman chaired a full committee.

Another change Speaker O'Neill brought to the House was the introduction of televised sessions. The liberal Democratic Study Group was pushing very hard to televise House sessions. As leader and then as speaker, O'Neill was always supportive of this initiative, but he listened to the concerns of committee chairs.

Many of the Southern barons who still ruled the House at the time were opposed. O'Neill's office heard these members make observations such as "This is going to change the institution. It's going to ruin the business that we're here to do for the people. It's going to interfere. We're going to have to change rules and procedures. How are the members going to respond to that? We're going to have a lot of prima donnas. We'll have no control over it." Other members shared these negative concerns.

Tip O'Neill heard them out but dismissed their worries to his staff, saying, "We will address all their concerns, but let's give it a shot and see how it works. We'll try a pilot program with closed-circuit TV and work out all the kinks first."

Speaker O'Neill authorized closed-circuit TV for a trial period of ninety days. His two key decisions—(1) that the camera would not pan the whole House floor but focus on the person who was speaking, and (2) that the speaker's office would control the broadcast— helped minimize the opposition.[209] He placed Charles "Charlie" Rose (North Carolina), a trusted colleague with ties across the spectrum of Democratic members, in the hot seat.

A legislative appropriation of $1.2 million funded the House purchase and installation of cameras and monitors.[210] Equipment was installed in the basement of the Capitol. The broadcast would be controlled through the speaker's office—in terms of what was televised, when it was televised, and how it was televised. Members accepted this pilot program, and House proceedings have been televised ever since.

Some of the first televised hearings in the House were the impeachment proceedings in the Judiciary Committee. This set a precedent of transparency that was perceived well by the public. It helped members to see the advantages. Americans at home could watch the Judiciary Committee impeachment hearings and see the brilliance of their elected representatives working for them.

Barbara Jordan (Texas) gave a powerfully compelling speech regarding Nixon's impeachment that was filmed:

> Earlier today, we heard the beginning of the Preamble to the Constitution of the United States: "We, the people." It's a very eloquent beginning. But when that document was completed on the seventeenth of September in 1787, I was not included in that "We, the people." I felt somehow for many years that George Washington and Alexander Hamilton just left me out by mistake. But through the process of amendment, interpretation, and court decision, I have finally been included in "We, the people."[211]

As a result, constituents in districts all over the country wanted to know what was happening—what was said—in Congress, and now they could.

The "prima donnas" did play to the cameras. They made more speeches and engaged in longer debates. Prior to television coverage, male Congress members generally wore the standard business attire—white shirt, conservative tie, and gray/brown/black suit. However, under the camera spotlights, the dress became somewhat more colorful. It was particularly apparent with women members who would dress in bright colors that popped on camera. Two colors predominated TV House coverage initially: blue and red. Congressmen wore blue shirts or a blue tie. Women representatives wore red, perceived as a power color, perhaps to build their confidence in a male-dominated House chamber. (Today, women members wear white in a show of unity and in homage to suffragists.)

***

One of the first items on Speaker O'Neill's change agenda was to create the strongest ethics of any legislative body in the world. Scandals involving members—mostly financial—had transpired from time to time. As a result, an ethics commission, chaired by David Obey (Wisconsin) and formed when O'Neill was majority leader, reported recommendations to the House.

The report offered several recommendations, which were implemented: it changed the honorarium level; it changed how much members could earn in outside income; it revoked the franking privilege for a certain period before elections; it eliminated unauthorized accounts; and it required disclosure of income, assets, and liabilities.[212] This was the first time the House had limited honorariums and outside incomes. Today, ethics for public officials have placed limitations beyond what O'Neill advocated, but such a strong ethics package was unheard of at that time.

Speaker O'Neill was serious about ethics. Not only did his package implement ethical standards to follow, but it also enabled House members to protect themselves. It passed the House, and Speaker O'Neill created a special Rules Committee structure to enforce it, making the ethics reform a real tiger with biting teeth.

One of his responsibilities as speaker was control over all special and joint committee appointments. This included the select committee on intelligence (which would later investigate Russian collusion in the 2016 election), to which he appointed his close friend from Massachusetts, Edward Boland, as chairman. Tip O'Neill made the Rules Committee *his* committee, in the sense of controlling all appointments to it while he was speaker. He consolidated more power in the speaker's office through the Steering and Policy Committee, in terms of committee assignments and working with the committee chairs to develop the party agenda.

As speaker, he became involved more in foreign policy than he had as whip (except for, of course, the Vietnam issue). The House Speaker is chief protocol officer of the legislative branch, chief parliamentarian of the House, and chief administrator of the House. He or she is the political leader of the majority party, which controls the House. Furthermore, the House

Speaker is second in line to the presidency after the Vice President. If anything happens to the President and Vice President, the House Speaker is sworn in as president.

As the chief protocol officer for the legislative branch, the Speaker often met with foreign leaders on official visits to the Capitol. Two foreign policy issues stand out during O'Neill's speakership in the 1970s: the Camp David Accords in 1978 and Northern Ireland in 1979.

O'Neill shared with his staff a story, not in any history book, that President Carter had told the House leadership after the Camp David Accords had been signed by Egyptian President Anwar Sadat and Israeli Prime Minister Menachem Begin. "How did you get them to reach an agreement?" O'Neill had asked Carter. The President said it was one of the toughest negotiations in the world. These two nations hated each other from generations of enmity. Just look in the Bible: the children of Israel were slaves in Egypt before Moses delivered them from the land of the Pharaohs in the thirteenth century BCE.[213] This conflict was deep-rooted and age-old.

President Carter said that getting the two leaders to be civil to each other was an effort. Several times, one of them had been angry enough to walk out. However, as the discussions and negotiations ensued, one of them would mention their grandchildren. President Carter, President Sadat, and Prime Minister Begin were all proud grandfathers, and they would often bring up the subject of grandchildren.

At one point, it dawned on the two bitter enemies almost simultaneously: No matter how they felt about each other or how long the conflict had lasted, the two leaders had the capacity to prevent their grandchildren from facing each other in war. They had the power through negotiation to prevent the killing of their grandchildren. President Carter said whenever the negotiation stalemated or looked like it was going to break up, they would start talking about the grandchildren again.[214]

Although this story didn't involve Speaker O'Neill directly, it seemed as though President Carter had taken a page out of Tip's own book. A natural mediator, O'Neill often had to find common ground between two opponents to achieve a compromise. And he knew how to defuse tension when a flare-up seemed inevitable. When Israeli Prime Minister Begin later visited the House, O'Neill mentioned Begin's grandchildren. "We know you're a proud grandfather," he said, inferring the human-interest story behind the Camp David Accords, signed for the sake of the Israeli and Egyptian grandchildren and future generations.

As speaker, O'Neill felt most strongly about his ancestral home, Ireland, and what, if anything, he could do to try to bring about peace there. He was speaker at the height of the Troubles; the IRA (Irish Republican Army) was responsible for bombings, assassinations, and other violent attacks. O'Neill wanted to determine the key players in Northern Ireland, the Republic of Ireland, and the United Kingdom and whether there was an interest in pursuing peace. The Republic of

Ireland was starting to turn around because of its membership in the European Union. O'Neill thought that this timing might promote peace talks.

He had the opportunity to go to Ireland as the highest-ranking official in the U.S. government since President Kennedy in 1963. (This was before President Ronald Reagan's visit in 1984.) O'Neill journeyed to Northern Ireland and met with all the leaders—Protestant, Catholic, and otherwise—including John Hume, the great Northern Ireland leader. Again, this visit brought out Speaker O'Neill's uncanny ability to judge character. When he went to Egypt, before the Camp David Accords, he had met Anwar Sadat and said, "If we're ever going to bring about peace in the Middle East, Anwar Sadat is the one who is able to do it." Likewise, when he met John Hume, he said, "If we're ever going to see peace in Northern Ireland and stop all this fighting and killing, it's going to be because of John Hume." Again, O'Neill had been prophetic; John Hume was instrumental in the Good Friday Agreement.

O'Neill went to Northern Ireland for three reasons: First, to ascertain the key players. Second, to see if an interest existed among the players to end the violence. Did they really want peace? They did in fact, but they didn't know how to work together to achieve it, and they were not quite ready in 1979. And third, he wanted to make it clear that he was not an imperial Irish American who would impose any scheme or support any American interference. America wasn't going to impose anything. This was work to be done by the

Irish and the British. He expressed great and sincere concern that his country wanted all sides to achieve peace and would do everything it could to help facilitate a move in that direction.

President Bill Clinton sent former Senate Majority Leader George Mitchell to negotiate the Good Friday Agreement for Northern Ireland in 1998. Mitchell gave great credit to Speaker O'Neill for starting the Irish peace process. The fact that such a high-ranking official of the United States took the time and the energy to visit and to listen to all the parties involved laid the groundwork for a future peace.

***

Majority Whip, Majority Leader, and Speaker—Thomas P. O'Neill was a change agent in every way. He led the caucus fight to end the Vietnam War; he embraced the abolition of the automatic seniority system for committee chairs, which opened up subcommittees; he changed the role of the Steering and Policy Committee; he instituted a workable plan to televise House sessions; and he implemented a far-reaching ethics bill. All of these changes were integral elements of the democratization of the House at the time. And, since 1967, he had stood firm in his stance against the Vietnam War.

Under his leadership, Tip O'Neill sought to usher in a new era to reassert the House's rightful voice in matters of war and peace. Gone were the days when Sam Rayburn would go to the White House and say,

"You tell us what you want us to do. Partisan politics stops at the water's edge. Tell us what you need in foreign policy, defense, war—whatever—and we'll get it to your desk for a signature." No longer did the President as commander in chief yield absolute supremacy in all matters of foreign policy. Congress would reclaim its constitutional right to declare war and, in so doing, to end war.

CHAPTER 17

The House's Rightful Role Restored?

Before this narrative concludes, it will revisit the 92nd Congress once more. In 1972, because of the initiative of one man, the House of Representatives had the opportunity to vote for the first time on termination of the Vietnam War in the standard legislative process.

The O'Neill caucus directive enabled the House to voice its will on an end-the-war amendment with a date certain, reported out of the Foreign Affairs Committee. Even though the issue was clouded on the House floor by the controversy over the change of date, explicit instructions from the Democratic caucus requiring the House Foreign Affairs Committee to act set the stage going forward. It signaled significant progress in a House chamber that had been unwilling to challenge the President to end the war and disinclined to restore the House's rightful role on issues of war and peace.

The subsequent votes by the House Foreign Affairs Committee responded, in part, to the caucus directive. Yet the committee fell short of its obligation in two instances: it failed to meet the thirty-day timetable to act on the caucus resolution, and it neglected to change in committee the unworkable deadline for disengagement from Vietnam. At times, the Congress—at work in committees—can move legislative initiatives with deliberate speed; at other times, the Congress works at a snail's pace. Unfortunately, the Foreign Affairs Committee chose the long-drawn-out action, and that negligence precipitated the no-win challenge on the House floor. The outcome was ill-fated and not at all what O'Neill and the doves had anticipated or desired.

However, the O'Neill-Gibbons caucus resolution was a fascinating political accomplishment on its merits. In its response to the O'Neill caucus initiative, in over a four-month timeframe, the House played out various factors in its standard legislative process. Such factors as party organization and leadership, House rules and procedures, timing, and personalities were keenly present. One cannot fully comprehend congressional action on a bill, resolution, or amendment without reflecting upon some of these significant factors. The O'Neill caucus initiative forced the House to consider, at the minimum, what power the House rightfully holds to terminate an unpopular, immoral war like Vietnam; it also helped the House to strategize, sketch, paint, and display its legislative action.

Perhaps the most important political contributions to the development of successful legislative policy are party organization and leadership management of the majority party that controls the Congress. In the early days of the 92nd Congress, the Democrats, with 255 members, held a significant majority over the 180 Republicans in the House.[215] But throughout this whole process, both in the Democratic caucus and during House floor consideration of the Morgan-Hamilton provision to the foreign aid bill, no visible top majority party leadership position existed on the issue. Speaker Albert and Majority Leader Boggs consistently refused to announce their positions publicly. They remained indecisive almost until the caucus vote on June 10, adopting the O'Neill resolution, and the House vote on August 10, defeating the Morgan-Hamilton provision.

As the two consummate elected leaders of the House Democrats, Speaker Albert and Leader Boggs were looking for a constructive and responsible congressional alternative to the Administration's policy. O'Neill offered them that alternative with his resolution in the caucus. Once they gave him their verbal commitment, they stuck to it, despite Edmondson's impulsive move to offer a substitute. Four months later, during House floor consideration of the Morgan-Hamilton-Whalen amendment with a December deadline, Albert and Boggs saw another responsible and realistic vote fulfilling the caucus charge. But neither one, following the House floor defeat of that amendment, would support the impractical October deadline of Section 13.

Albert and Boggs should not be criticized for their vote to strike Section 13, the Morgan-Hamilton provision with the October deadline. Hale Boggs articulately pointed out in his House floor remarks that, as one to whom the Democratic members of the House had invested a large and unassailable degree of responsibility, he could not in good conscience vote to enact an ineffectual provision. The Morgan-Hamilton provision (Section 13) could not be implemented; it would reflect poorly on the House of Representatives, which was trying to assert its rightful and coequal role to end the war, and it would be misinterpreted by North Vietnam and U.S. adversaries all over the world.

Yet neither one of these supreme House leaders gave any outward assistance to obtain House floor passage of the Morgan-Hamilton-Whalen change of date. That is where the two leaders deserve criticism. As John Gardner of Common Cause articulated without reservation, fault can be found in their indecision and unwillingness to take a firm stand to voice their support for the Morgan-Hamilton provision as amended by Whalen. The position of the two top leaders should have been to unequivocally accept the Whalen floor amendment. Furthermore, they should have ordered a whip count on Section 13. A whip count of the Democratic members would have signaled, most likely in advance of the House floor vote, the problem the issue-oriented liberals had with the date of October 1.

Although they personally supported the Morgan-Hamilton-Whalen proposal, Albert and Boggs refused to force a party position on the end-the-war issue. They did not want to risk alienating conservative members, who opposed any congressional interference with the presidential power to end the Vietnam War. Besides, it was an emotional vote of personal conviction, and their desire to end the war was not strong enough to take an unwavering stand on the House floor. This refusal by the two top Democratic leaders left an almost insurmountable leadership vacuum on the issue.

Decisiveness and willingness to take risks are the marks of good and effective leadership. Congressional leaders should be steadfast change agents. If leaders do not lead on an issue, they are merely preserving the status quo. Without the determination to be a catalyst for change, especially on a matter of House prerogative, a leadership vacuum develops.

Since a top leadership vacuum existed on the Vietnam issue in the House of Representatives, O'Neill intuitively recognized the necessity for party leadership in the caucus. He knew it could not be realized merely from a faction of liberal Democrats. O'Neill, as majority whip and as the leader of the House doves since 1967, satisfied and filled that leadership vacuum. Even though his decision to take a stand potentially created further tension with Albert and Boggs, he could not act otherwise.

Moreover, to lead, even at great risk, was ingrained in Tip O'Neill's political persona. It was a key to his political success both in Massachusetts politics and in the Congress. He never ran away from a controversial issue in his life. As a leader, he seldom hesitated while others acted when he knew it was the right action to take.

Compelled by political necessity to introduce a more general proposal, separate and apart from

Drinan's, O'Neill had the courage and foresight to assume the mantle of leadership where a definite vacuum existed. He willingly took on the potential consequences of political disaffection from his two leaders. He weighed the options, made his decision based on passionate and moral conviction, and carefully completed his homework to see his resolution adopted by the caucus.

Timing is another significant factor in the legislative process. Part of O'Neill's decision was based on his political awareness that the opportunity was ripe for a majority of the Democrats to support a resolution to mandate the House Foreign Affairs Committee to act. The time had come for a supreme effort on behalf of the antiwar cause.

O'Neill understood well the mood of the House. His political insight told him that the Democrats would flatly reject the Drinan proposal. They would be unwilling to put themselves on record in favor of specific legislation that would cut off funds to terminate American military operations in Indochina. Even the Senate, far more dovish than the House, had not been willing to take that drastic step as late as 1972.

Indeed, the timing was ripe for a major breakthrough in the efforts of the antiwar bloc to obtain full House approval of legislation to terminate the war in Vietnam. The stars seemed to align for the House doves. It was an election year, the Democrats were dissatisfied with President Nixon's Vietnamization policy and management of the air war, and the impetus for a partisan effort was present.

Of course, O'Neill's action at the caucus was motivated in part by a desire to obtain full House approval of an antiwar amendment—a seemingly unsurmountable effort. Yet that consideration was secondary to the major problem that had to be resolved first: that is, how to enable the House to voice its will directly on the Vietnam polemic through the standard legislative process. To resolve that problem required the caucus to determine the best approach to mandate a House committee to meet, deliberate, draft, and report out an end-the-war measure that had been introduced by a member of the House.

No, the House had never acted in the standard legislative process on this issue, but that was the main purpose of the O'Neill caucus resolution. Once the measure had been reported from the Foreign Affairs Committee, the House could work its ultimate will. At least the House would have this unique opportunity to act on its own end-the-war amendment, rather than just mirroring or reacting to a Senate proposal.

A third and equally significant contribution to the success of O'Neill's caucus resolution was the art of compromise—the foundation of the American political process. O'Neill had to take the fight away from the issue-oriented liberals. He had to offer a more general provision that could receive a majority of Democratic support yet was strong enough to give the House an opportunity to voice its official word on the Vietnam War. It had to be an amendment with real teeth in it—not a paper tiger, like the Stratton and Edmondson proposals, which could be ignored easily.

Although O'Neill had co-sponsored the Drinan bill and supported congressional action to cut off funds to terminate the war, he knew that the majority of the Democratic members of the House would not take that irreversible step. Also, he understood that he would not secure support for the Drinan resolution from the two leaders, Albert and Boggs, not to mention Chairman Morgan. They would not be willing to take that extreme a confrontation with the Administration. A compromise—a more general provision with wider appeal that still mandated the House Foreign Affairs Committee to act—was in order. It was the only measure the caucus would be ready to adopt that could be supported by Albert, Boggs, and Morgan.

It is important to recognize that all the invaluable information on the shortcomings of Drinan's proposal—too specific legislation, clash of personalities, dubious leadership support—came from careful research by O'Neill's whip staff. It was through diligent staff work that O'Neill learned about the DSG resolution, which he readily saw as the strongest possible resolution the caucus could adopt. One cannot underestimate the briefing and backup material that a staff prepares for a member of Congress; often, a legislator is only as effective as his or her staff's efforts.

Personalities form another significant contribution to the legislative process. The interacting personalities of Tip O'Neill, Father Drinan, and Ole Doc Morgan, as well as all the Democratic members of the House and the members of the Foreign Affairs Committee, were prime factors in the process. One cannot divorce personalities from politics and policies. Only O'Neill with the respect and following he commanded from his Democratic colleagues in the House could gain support from the leadership. Only O'Neill, the best-liked man in the House, could usurp authority in the caucus from the issue-oriented liberals without alienating anyone to formulate a successful outcome. If it were not for O'Neill's key whip position, personal leadership, and diligent homework, the O'Neill-Gibbons resolution would not have passed the caucus. Instead, the Democrats might have adopted the watered-down version proposed by Edmondson, which in effect did nothing.

Four months ensued from adoption of the O'Neill caucus resolution until House floor action on Section 13. When victory seemed close at hand in August, the issueoriented liberals were unwilling to compromise on changing the date certain with the Whalen amendment. Their refusal resulted in a vote that effectively killed the end-the-war amendment.

Perhaps if the liberals had compromised on the Morgan-Hamilton provision as amended by Whalen, the end-the-war amendment might have had a chance for passage. At least, as O'Neill and his legislative assistant analyzed later, the vote would have demonstrated the strongest showing in the House of an attempt to end the war. If the vote had been closer, it would have been so much more meaningful as the first time the House had such a unique opportunity to work its will on the Vietnam issue through the standard legislative process.

The Morgan-Hamilton amendment promotes an appreciation for committee action, strategy, and timing. First and foremost, the personality of Chairman Morgan—his low-profile yet cunning demeanor—set the tone for the Foreign Affairs Committee deliberation on the issue. The fact that Chairman Morgan felt bound by the caucus resolution indicated that the committee would take action. Although the committee was mandated to act, the caucus was powerless to impose any realistic penalty upon Democratic members of the Foreign Affairs Committee who did not support the majority position, nor could it penalize the Chairman for inaction within the thirty-day mandate to act.

Prior to the caucus directive, the House of Representatives never had the opportunity to vote on an end-the-Vietnam-War measure reported by the Foreign Affairs Committee. Doc Morgan, a hawk, had been successful in blocking consideration of any antiwar legislation by his committee. Though the majority of the Democrats on the committee were doves, the Chairman's position on the issue was significant to prevent the committee from reporting out a congressional initiative to terminate American involvement in Indochina.

Once the caucus had acted, the position of leadership was passed from O'Neill to Chairman Morgan, who would determine the course of legislation through his committee. The onus was then on the Foreign Affairs Committee to work its will. O'Neill was not a member of the committee; he had to respect the Chairman's timetable and defer action to the committee. Oh yes, he followed the action closely and was kept informed by Lee Hamilton, his zone whip.

Once the beginning of June rolled around, O'Neill reminded Morgan of his commitment to follow through on the directive from the caucus. Morgan then took quick action by calling an executive session of the Democrats on the committee within twenty days of the caucus directive. But he needed a little more push from O'Neill to follow through with a full committee executive session. O'Neill gave Morgan that impetus, although the committee did not act until June 13, two months after the caucus action.

As O'Neill put it, at least the House had something with which to work, albeit a resolution supporting the President's Indochina policy. No one seemed concerned that Chairman Morgan had not acted within the thirty days mandated by the caucus directive.

The rules and procedures of the legislative process in the House of Representatives were important for O'Neill, a masterful parliamentarian from years of experience as a member of the House Rules Committee. He consistently used a parliamentary situation to his advantage to obtain the most favorable vote for his caucus resolution. While the Edmondson move surprised O'Neill and temporarily thwarted his advantage, he was ready for a procedural maneuver if Gibbons were allowed to offer his amendment before a vote could be taken on the O'Neill resolution.

The last but most important factor in the legislative process is the issue itself. Here, the timely issue was ending the war in Vietnam, but the real issue was larger.

Even though a majority of Democrats, 71 percent, supported an end-the-war amendment that set a date certain for termination of American involvement, the House was not ready to accept on August 10, 1972, the MorganHamilton provision because the issue was clouded over the date. Thus, the House did not have a clear vote on a realistic end-the-war amendment reported out of the Foreign Affairs Committee with a date certain. In rejecting it, the House, once again, as in 1971, had given its approval to the lengthy disengagement steps being taken by the President.

The larger issue before the House was an opportunity to voice its will for the first time on the Indochina polemic in the standard legislative process. O'Neill believed that the Congress, which has the constitutional right to declare war and the right to provide for the conduct and continuation of the war through the authorization and appropriations processes, also has the right to end the war. Yet the House of Representatives, by defeating the Morgan-Hamilton provision to the foreign aid bill of 1972, in essence failed to use its power of the purse to cut off funding. Thereby, the House continued its support for the position that the President is the ultimate authority to terminate American involvement in the Indochina hostilities.

This story of the O'Neill caucus resolution explores at a given time in the history of America's experiment in democracy the legislative interplay of political leadership, timing, compromise, and decisiveness that advances public policy. Perhaps the two most important factors that led to the adoption of the O'Neill caucus resolution are the politics of personalities and political management of the majority from the key position of the majority whip.

It is the remarkable story of one man's attempt to accomplish a milestone in the history of the American legislative process. For in the year 1972, because of the initiative and leadership of Thomas P. "Tip" O'Neill Jr., the House of Representatives was given the opportunity to have its official voice heard in the standard legislative process on the critical issue of war and peace to determine continued American involvement in the Vietnam War.

Lay It on the Table

Epilogue

❀

The late 1960s and early 1970s were tumultuous times in American history. In city streets, on college campuses, and in Washington, people across America protested: young people, waiting to be drafted, demonstrated against the Vietnam War; Martin Luther King Jr. lived and died fighting for civil rights and justice for Black Americans; women burned bras, demanding equal rights; students seized college buildings, agitating for more love, not war. These protests brought a measure of change to America, breaking down some barriers that prevented women and minorities from seizing opportunities to realize their potential—from experiencing the American dream.

Many of these same inequities exist today, and people still strive to overcome; women march to demand economic justice, reproductive rights, and the Equal Rights Amendment to the Constitution; Black Lives Matter is a social movement that protests white supremacy, police brutality, and racially motivated violence against Black people. These protests continue today to advance the democracy our forefathers ideally

envisioned and engrained in our American conscious-
ness, creating a uniquely American culture.

As Václav Havel, the Czech Republic's first demo-
cratically elected president, pointed out to Congress on
February 22, 1990:

> Democracy, in the full sense of the word, will al-
> ways be no more than an ideal. One may approach
> it as one would the horizon . . . but it can never be
> fully attained. . . . You . . . are merely approach-
> ing democracy. You have thousands of problems of
> all kinds, as other countries do. But you have one
> great advantage: You have been approaching de-
> mocracy uninterruptedly for more than 200 years,
> and your journey toward the horizon has never
> been disrupted by a totalitarian system.[216]

These democratic ideals, etched eternally in the
Declaration of Independence, consist first in the equality of opportunity—"all men are created equal." Of
course, our founding documents left out women and
people of color then, as Representative Barbara Jor-
don so poignantly articulated into living rooms where
Americans watched the House televised impeachment
hearings. Equality of opportunity is the right to a level
playing field to pursue our aspirations, whatever we
want to do, and to go as far as we desire—not allowing
anyone to prevent us from achieving our goals.

The second ideal is "life, liberty, and the pursuit
of happiness"—the right to control our own destinies
as free individuals. Some Americans, like former First

Lady Michelle Obama, believe that once one walks across that threshold of opportunity, an obligation, a responsibility, a duty ensues to make sure others can cross that threshold too.[217]

Tip O'Neill embodied these two Revolutionary principles, calling them "opportunity and achievement": *opportunity*, meaning an equal playing field, and *achievement*, meaning "work and wages" as achieved through the capitalist system. He described *work and wages* as the right to a job, the ability to work, and the capacity to earn a decent wage to support one's family. That was why he supported many of the liberal causes of his day, such as unions, minimum wage increases, and health benefits.

The 1970s and 1980s were rewarding years to work on Capitol Hill. As a staff person, I engaged with many young people in positions of influence who were committed to the House as an institution and conveyed such refreshing and innovative ideas. We learned so much from each other. We bounced ideas back and forth. And we respected each other's ideas, even if they were very different from our own. Different was not viewed as inferior or deficient; it was respected for what it was—different. And we tried, despite our differences, to reach an ultimate agreement—to get to *yes*.

Unlike many who belong to the House today, we asked meaningful questions and found answers: *How do we work things out? How do we negotiate? How do we compromise? How do we build relationships?* Today, progressives do not build relationships with moderates among Democrats; Republican members of the Freedom and Tea Party caucuses do not build relationships with moderates in the Republican Party. Too few members—and staff who reflect members' attitudes—seek bipartisan cooperation and actually reach across the aisle, or within the ideological divides of their own political party, to advance legislation.

In my time on Capitol Hill, many members stayed in Washington during the week because their spouses moved to the Washington area to live with them. Their children all attended the same schools. The members and their spouses socialized and got to know each other. They went out together after work. If one socializes or develops a friendly relationship with another, it is much more difficult to attack each other. It is not this way today.

I remember the seventies and eighties as a time when Senators Ted Kennedy (Massachusetts) and Orrin Hatch (Utah)—diametrically opposed in ideology—could work together on issues that benefited American citizens. It was a time when Majority Leader/Speaker Tip O'Neill (Massachusetts) and Minority Leaders Jerry Ford (Michigan), John Rhodes (Arizona), or Bob Michel (Illinois) could come together and work a compromise that was in the best interest of the public. A sprit of collegiality, cooperation, and compromise pervaded the House under O'Neill's leadership. He personified a commitment, an energy, a willingness to work out solutions and to negotiate until the House could get to yes.

It was a point in time when the House was *approaching* the democracy Czech President Havel described in his speech to Congress and what our Founding Fathers envisioned. The popularity and respect O'Neill commanded helped him to be the change agent he was and to democratize the House. His leadership instilled great pride to serve as a member of the House of Representatives and fostered honor and privilege to work as a staff person. Sadly, that spirit is missing four decades later.

I believe TV was a major factor in changing that House floor spirit. Anytime an institution introduces new technology, unintended negative consequences evolve. Newt Gingrich, a Republican from Georgia, was elected to the speakership in 1995. In my view, he manipulated the TV coverage so that conservative Republican members could take back the ideological and numerical control of the House. Gingrich believed the House of Representatives had gone too far in the direction of the liberals and DSG members. He and other conservative Republican members used special orders and the one-minute speeches to lash out against Democratic members. Before TV coverage of House floor action, one-minute speeches at the beginning of the House sessions and special orders at the end were used mainly to honor a member's constituents: an Eagle Scout, a Gold Star mother, someone important who had passed away in their district. Seldom, if ever, did a member lash out against another member.

Today's Congress is dysfunctional, and bipartisan cooperation in the House is so endangered, it is virtually extinct. Compromise is sadly lacking. In the seventies and eighties, the House was a wonderful place to work; whether Democrat or Republican, conservative or liberal, members tried to work together for the best interests of the constituents they represented. Differing opinions and trade-offs gave the House a sense of balance and fairness. They understood give and take— they knew they would not get everything they wanted, but they were willing to cooperate. *Compromise* was not a dirty word.

Members of both parties would fight the good fight, arguing against the opponents on the issue, yet 75 to 80 percent of the issues were bipartisan. They did not engage in excessive partisan wrangling. They never took things so personally that the fight became dirty. If a member proposed a bad idea, other members would not call that member pathetic or ignorant. No one used language that was derogatory, mean-spirited, or personally offensive. Members did not verbally bash each other; rather, they opposed the issue itself and reasoned why they thought it was a bad idea.

Beginning in the mid-1990s, floor action became very personalized—and that was due to messaging, provided by TV and later social media. It was no longer a question of how we can use the legislative process and work together to get to yes. It was how we can best malign the other person and get the message out to make that person look bad. This kind of behavior began under Speaker Gingrich's leadership, and it is carrying on today. It's unfortunate because I believe it is one of the unintended consequences of greater transparency provided by televised House coverage.

***

One positive change in the modern era is more women in the House and greater respect for women representatives. In the early 1970s, women—members and professional staff—were tolerated but clearly pariahs in the House. You will remember the Democratic Cloakroom was like a neighborhood boys' club in the seventies—"girls not welcome here." The few professional women who worked on Capitol Hill tended to commiserate together.

One woman who was a great mentor to me was Janice Lipsen, who worked for Speaker Carl Albert. She also had House floor privileges for a period of time, and she and I worked together. We bonded and shared wonderful experiences on the House floor. I can remember talking to women members as well as congressmen—we talked to everybody. Sometimes, Janice and I would be talking to one or two women members, and some of the male representatives would come up and say, "Oh, what are you girls cooking up? Are you conspiring against us?"

"Why would we be conspiring against you? It's just girl talk."

They'd look at us—not quite believing—say, "Oh," and walk away. It was funny. Three or more women chatting on the House floor caused such concern among the congressmen. Years later, during my freshman year in the Massachusetts State Senate, I was talking to two other women state senators. Male state senators approached us and said, "Are you three conspiring against us?" I thought, *I can't believe this. It's happening here in Massachusetts ten years later—*

the same thing that happened on the House floor in Washington!

Perhaps the most discriminatory House offense to women staffers was, of course, pay—in terms of how members felt about the salary we professional women received. Now, one particular female professional was Jonalyn Cullen, who was the staff counsel for the Rules Committee. She and I were very close. She was from Mississippi and so was William Colmer, the Rules Committee chairman. Colmer really liked her, and Tip O'Neill did too. (She later worked for Rep. Trent Lott [Mississippi] when he became minority whip.)

Everybody on the Rules Committee worked with her and found her professional, competent, and extremely knowledgeable about the House process. She worked with Democrats, Republicans, conservatives, and liberals. She and I were miles apart ideologically. I was a moderate liberal from Massachusetts. She was a Mississippi conservative Democrat (which meant she was a Republican in Democratic clothing from Mississippi). But we got along, and we worked together for the best interest of the House. She was always supportive, helpful, and informative. Members liked her—both Democrats and Republicans.

I remember when a book of employee salaries was published and some of the congressmen were on the floor perusing it. Members of the Rules Committee said, "Did you see Jonalyn's salary?"

They looked at me as I approached to see what the figure was. I said, "What's wrong with that?"

They said, "Well, she's a woman. She shouldn't be earning this kind of money." Then I think they realized they had said this to another woman who was also a professional staff person.

I certainly did not earn what Jonalyn did at that point, by any means. I froze for a minute. Then I said, "You all like her, don't you? You work well with her? Don't you think she deserves what she's worth? She earns every bit of it." And I walked away. The subject never came up again—at least not in my presence— but that attitude prevailed toward women staff.

***

As I come to the end of this story about the O'Neill caucus resolution to end the Vietnam War and subsequent House action, I look back at the Congress then and the Congress today, and I see many differences. But when I think about the policy of war and peace then as opposed to now, and the determination of U.S. intervention in foreign wars, it feels unsettling and familiar.

I have no doubt that the O'Neill caucus resolution to terminate the Vietnam War was the right course of action for that moment in history. Vietnam War demonstrations were different from domestic protests and required an immediate response in 1972. They symbolized a war that was wrong: it was a war the U.S. had never officially declared, a war with an unclear mission and no end game, and a war that we needed to exit posthaste. But did we learn from the lessons of our mistakes in Vietnam?

Some of you who are old enough will remember the messy evacuation of American personnel in helicopters from the rooftop of the U.S. embassy as Saigon fell to the communists. The evacuation seemed chaotic—the images unsettling. It appeared as if no preplanning had occurred for the inevitable fall of South Vietnam in 1975 without continued U.S. military support alongside the South Vietnamese army after 1973. Yet neither Democrats nor Republicans criticized President Ford's evacuation execution.

Any exodus, when withdrawing from a losing war, is not possible without chaos. Summing up the Vietnam War debacle, Mike Mansfield, former Senate majority leader, stated: "The cost was 55,000 dead, 303,000 wounded, $150 billion. It was unnecessary, uncalled-for, it wasn't tied to our security or a vital interest. It was just a misadventure in a part of the world which we should have kept our nose out of."[218]

History is repeating itself today as we disengage from Afghanistan, America's longest war of twenty years. We sent our military into Afghanistan after the 9/11 terrorist attacks in 2001 with the idea that we would fight the terrorists on their own stomping grounds, and to keep the war away from our land and our civilians. But then we didn't leave. It was finally decided that 2021 would be the year to pull out, and that withdrawal from Afghanistan is unfolding as I write the last pages of this book, bringing a nearly fifty-year-old story to the present with a vivid sense of déjà vu.

The media has coined our withdrawal from Afghanistan as "botched," the worst foreign policy debacle since Vietnam.[219] Our intelligence agencies seemed unable to predict the swift retreat of the Afghan government and its army; no one anticipated the unprecedented quick collapse of all we had invested in Afghanistan for twenty years. Like Vietnam, the Afghan army could not sustain the war effort without U.S. combat troops fighting alongside. It had neither the will to defend its corrupt government nor the requisite courage to fight the Taliban enemy despite billions of dollars in American equipment and training.[220]

Once President Joe Biden set the deadline of U.S. withdrawal for August 31, 2021, and began to bring American troops home, the Taliban advanced. Afghanistan's corrupt government, which we supported, collapsed as its president fled the country. The Taliban seized each provincial capital over eleven days. Within forty-eight hours, after controlling much of the country, it marched in and took control of the capital city of Kabul with virtually no opposition.

Americans and Afghans fled to Kabul's airport, still under U.S. control, to escape the brutality of the Taliban and the return of reprisals and restrictions under the Islamic Sharia law, which is highly discriminatory toward women. The scenes at Kabul's airport included babies being lifted over concrete barriers and razor wire, Afghan women and children running along the tarmac, and men clinging to the edges of U.S. cargo planes as they took off. Each plane carried hundreds of Americans and Afghan refugees desperate to flee the country rather than stay to be hunted down and likely killed by the Taliban.

Democrats and Republicans alike hold President Biden responsible for the "botched" withdrawal and evacuation of Americans and Afghans who assisted the Americans over the twenty-year occupation. A few Republicans are clamoring for Biden's resignation, suggesting he is unfit to be commander in chief. Yet these same critics fail to realize how the U.S. military fulfilled its role of colonial occupier, replacing the Russians in Afghanistan, just as we succeeded the French colonial power in Vietnam. Neither one of these U.S. interventions had an official declaration of war by the Congress. In both cases, the United States became the new colonial Western power occupying foreign peoples' lands.

Vietnam and Afghanistan have different cultures and customs from ours, and both were engaged in civil wars in which neighbor fought against neighbor from the same province or village. We sent our military to both countries to fight for noble goals—to eradicate communism in Vietnam, terrorism in Afghanistan. The enemy—the North Vietnamese and Viet Cong in Vietnam and the Taliban in Afghanistan—was never defeated. They all were too highly motivated, refreshed by a constant source of young recruits ready to fight us, the occupiers of their turf, as well as the corrupt government that garnered little popular support.[221] (Recall our own revolution, in which the ragged American army drove out the British colonial occupier, the world power of that era.)

In both wars, we expanded our original mission, adding nation-building in these two countries with completely different cultures from our own. This new mission would have never succeeded because we can't *make* any other country or government choose freedom and democracy, much less fight to keep it free and democratic. Military objectives must be more narrowly focused with a specific mission and quickly expedited; to occupy a country indefinitely makes the U.S. no better than the imperialists of old.

O'Neill was right in his efforts to lead the House in getting us out of Vietnam. He could not have predicted Afghanistan five decades later, but he knew we had no business continuing our operation in the midst of Vietnam's civil war, even if it were to contain communism. Our mission had become blurred and lofty. In addition to fighting communism, it morphed into utopian nation-building, in which we imposed our democratic values on a corrupt South Vietnamese government that had little popular support. Hindsight manifests its folly.

Perhaps the next time the United States intervenes in other lands, ostensibly to fight an "avatar of evil,"[222] it will go with a clearer mission, accomplish that mission speedily with necessary force, and withdraw just as quickly. Perhaps we will recognize at the outset that it will not be a complete victory and we will not change a nation's ideology to match ours. Perhaps if we follow Tip O'Neill's example, we will stop hemorrhaging American taxpayer dollars on a lost imperial cause.

***

America's Citadel of Freedom, the U.S. Capitol, resides on a hill in Washington, D.C. Inside sits the House of Representatives—the People's House. As Alexander Hamilton said, "It's here, sir, the people govern." It is the consummate chamber of democracy, the greatest elective body in the history of the world, where one must be elected to serve. One can be appointed president. One can be appointed vice president. One can be appointed to the U.S. Senate. Yet one must be elected to serve in the People's House. O'Neill was proud to serve his constituents there. To be duly sworn in eighteen times as an elected member of the People's House was a high honor indeed; to lead in the House was the noblest career achievement, which O'Neill never took for granted. It speaks volumes to his legacy in a remarkable thirty-six-year span of dedicated public service in the U.S. House of Representatives.

Although the U.S. Capitol appears the same, what happens inside its two chambers has certainly changed in the last fifty years—in some good ways and some bad. Foreign policy changes with each incoming Administration, but essentially, it's the same story over and again. Perhaps a Tip O'Neill of the twenty-first century will emerge from one of our fifty states, venture into our nation's capital, and lead us out of this quagmire toward a horizon of democracy. Then again, maybe not. But here is part of our history—*his* story. I lay it on the table, not to delay or delete it, but as an offering that we might take it for what it's worth—a decision made in a moment in time—and ultimately learn from it.

Endnotes

Preface

1   National Park Service, Springfield Armory, "History & Culture: The Forge of Innovation," https://www.nps.gov/spar/learn/historyculture/index.htm.

2   Jane Fenderson was the legislative assistant for Sen. Ed Muskie and later chief scheduler for First Lady Rosalynn Carter.

3   Judith Kurland later worked for Lt. Gov. Thomas P. O'Neill III, Tip O'Neill's son, before becoming the health commissioner for the city of Boston and chief of staff for Boston's Mayor Thomas Merino.

Chapter 1: Washington in April Unfurled

4   Democratic Study Group Fact Sheet 92-20, "Indochina Caucus Resolution," 4.

5   Ibid.

6   Ibid.

7   Ibid, 1.

8   The Harris Poll, The Washington Post, April 12, 1972.

9   Tip O'Neill, letter to Democratic members concerning Wednesday caucus, April 13, 1972. A Democratic caucus— a meeting of all House Democrats—was held the third Wednesday of each month to discuss matters of party policy and cooperation.

Chapter 2: The Hamlet Dilemma: To Lead or Not to Lead?

10 Tip O'Neill, conversation with legislative assistant, April 13, 1972.

11 Legislative assistant, in a memo to Tip O'Neill, April 18, 1972.

12 Hays was one of the most antagonistic members of the House toward liberal members like Robert Drinan and Bella Abzug; see chapter 11 for more about Wayne Hays.

13 Assistant Whip John McFall (California) was also a hawk, while Assistant Whip John Brademas (Indiana) was a dove.

14 Bill Arbogast and Carl Albert, remarks made at the Speaker's Press Conference, April 18, 1972.

Chapter 3: The Legislative Process and the Art of the Possible

15 History, Art, & Archives: United States House of Representatives, "Bill Hopper," https://history.house.gov/Collection/Listing/2004/2004-019-000/.

16 Woodrow Wilson, Congressional Government: A Study in American Politics (Boston: Houghton Mifflin, 1885), 79.

17 In 1972, all the committee chairpersons were men. Today, House committees are chaired by men and women and together called "chairs."

18 Congressional Institute, "Open House: How the House of Representatives Can Reinvigorate the Amendment Process," https://www.congressionalinstitute.org/open-house-how-the-house-of-representatives-can-reinvigorate-the-amendment-process/#_ednref27.

19 Wilson, Congressional Government, 102.

20 Since the rule changes in the 93rd Congress, markup sessions are now open to the public unless the members of the committee vote specifically to close the session on the day scheduled for the markup.

21 United States Senate, "Cloture," https://www.senate.gov/
artandhistory/history/common/generic/Origins_Cloture.htm.

22 Ibid.

Chapter 4: A New Order—The House Balks

23 James A. Robinson, *Congress and Foreign Policymaking: A Study in Legislative Influence and Initiative* (Homewood, Illinois.: Dorsey Press, 1962), 61–62.

24 *Congressional Quarterly Almanac,* 1962, 346.

25 The city of Berlin had been divided in 1961, when the Soviet Union built a wall separating communist-run East Germany from West Germany.

26 *CQ Almanac,* 1962, 346.

27 *Congress and the Nation, 1945–1964* (Washington: U.S. Government Printing Office, 1965), 130–131.

28 Ibid, 120–121; *CQ Almanac,* 1957, 573–574.

29 GovTrack, "H.J.Res. 117 (85th): Joint resolution to promote peace and stability in the Middle East," https://www.govtrack.us/congress/bills/85/hjres117/text.

30 *Congress and the Nation,* 120–121; *CQ Almanac,* 1957, 573–574.

31 *CQ Almanac,* 1957, 575–577.

32 *Congress and the Nation,* 138; "Transcript of Tonkin Gulf Resolution (1964)," https://www.ourdocuments.gov/doc.php?flash=false&doc=98&page=transcript.

33 Office of the Historian, "U.S. Involvement in the Vietnam War: the Gulf of Tonkin and Escalation, 1964," https://history.state.gov/milestones/1961-1968/gulf-of-tonkin.

34 History, Art, & Archives: United States House of Representatives, "Power to Declare War," https://history.house.gov/Institution/Origins-Development/War-Powers/.

35 *CQ Almanac,* 1964, 332.

36 Encyclopedia Britannica editors. "Gulf of Tonkin Resolution." *Encyclopedia Britannica*, July 29, 2021, https://www.britannica.com/event/Gulf-of-Tonkin-Resolution.

37 *Public Papers of the Presidents: Lyndon B. Johnson, Vol. II* (1963–1964), 946–947.

38 The War Powers Act and 2021 efforts to reenact it are discussed in chapter 15.

39 Clement Zablocki (Wisconsin), member of the House Foreign Affairs Committee, interview with the author, November 30, 1972.

40 Ibid. Senator Fulbright did not have the votes after President Johnson made his announcement not to seek reelection.

41 *Digest of Amendments* in the 91st and 92nd Congress limiting U.S. involvement in the Indochina War (Washington: Congressional Research Service), 5.

42 Ibid, 11. The amendment was later rejected in the House in a tabling motion.

43 Ibid, 33. This amendment passed the Senate, 72 to 22, and was adopted in the House as a conference report, becoming Public Law 21-652, Section 7.

44 Ibid, 26.

45 From conversations with aides to Speaker Albert and Majority Leader Boggs who shall remain anonymous. Speaker McCormack was likewise from that school of bipartisan cooperation in foreign policy.

46 *Digest of Amendments*, 9ff.

47 Ibid. The first vote, 57 to 42, occurred June 27, 1971, and had a nine-month deadline. The second vote, 57 to 38, occurred September 30, 1971, with a six-month deadline, since three months had already passed since the first vote.

48 Ibid, 38.

49 Democratic Study Group Fact Sheet 92-15, October 7, 1971, 5.

50 *Congressional Record*, June 17, 1971, H 5399; *Digest of Amendments*, 40.

51 Ibid, June 28, 1971, H 5943; *Digest of Amendments*, 9.

52 The number of nays should total 176, but the records show conflicting numbers, perhaps because one member changed his vote from nay to yea.

53 DSG Fact Sheet 92-15, "The Mansfield Amendment," October 7, 1971, 5.

54 *Digest of Amendments*, 39.

55 "Conferees Fail Again on Aid Bill," *The New York Times*, December 4, 1971.

56 Technically, the House Appropriations Committee could have also processed a germane amendment cutting off funds to a supplemental or continuing appropriation bill or to the annual defense and foreign aid appropriation bills.

Chapter 5: Core Beliefs: People Like to be Asked

57 John A. Farrell, *Tip O'Neill and the Democratic Century* (Boston: Little, Brown and Company, 2001).

58 "Biographical Note," *Tip O'Neill Congressional Papers, 1936–1994*, John J. Burns Library, Boston College.

59 Eric Zorn, "Democrats can take a few tips from O'Neill," *Chicago Tribune*, July 25, 2004.

60 Rep. Edward P. Boland and Rep. James Burke, colleagues who served with O'Neill in the Massachusetts State Legislature, interviews with the author.

61 Michael Sletcher, "The Loyalty of Educators and Public Employees: Opposition to Loyalty Oaths in Twentieth-Century Massachusetts and the U.S. Supreme Court," *The Massachusetts Historical Review*, Vol. 12, 2010.

62 Rep. William Jennings Bryan Dorn, seconding speech for O'Neill's nomination as majority leader, Democratic Caucus, January 2, 1973.

63 Democratic colleague who shall remain anonymous, quoted by David Scheffer, "How to Make Friends and Influence People," *Harvard Crimson*, February 12, 1973.

64 Tip O'Neill, quoted by Scheffer, "How to Make Friends," *Harvard Crimson*.

65 Ibid.

66 Tip O'Neill, remarks to the press.

67 Michael Peck, "The Vietnam War Almost Ended in 1972 (Then the U.S. Navy and Air Force Stepped In)," *The National Interest*, October 26, 2019, https://nationalinterest. org/blog/buzz/vietnam-war-almost-ended-1972-then-us-navy-and-air-force-stepped-91316.

Chapter 6: The Whip (Office) in Action

68 In 1971, deputy whips, chief deputy whips, and assistant whips did not exist; they came later.
69 The House Democratic Cloakroom, https://democratic-cloakroom.house.gov/about.
70 A decade later, twenty-one women members served. The influx of women elected to the House grew in the 1990s and into the twenty-first century. Today, in the 117th Congress, more than a hundred women serve in the House. For more information about women in the House, see chapter 16.

Chapter 7: "Let Us Be Responsible for Ending the War"

71 Sam Stratton, resolution offered at the Democratic Caucus, *Journal of Proceedings of Democratic Caucus*, April 19, 1972.
72 O'Neill and Stratton frequently got into many vituperative colloquies during the whip coffees and on the floor whenever the Vietnam issue was discussed.
73 Common Cause staff, telephone interview with the author, May 15, 1973.
74 At the time of the O'Neill caucus resolution, the number of DSG members was 140.
75 Ibid.
76 Common Cause lobbyists, interview with the author, April 18, 1972.
77 Tip O'Neill, letter to Democratic members re. Wednesday caucus, April 13, 1972.

78 This was in part because of the mantle of executive privilege that Nixon put around all his White House aides.

79 Sonny Montgomery, comment made to the author.

80 Tip O'Neill, remarks to the press.

81 Preamble and Rules adopted by the Democratic Caucus, January 18, 1971.

82 Leadership letter to Democratic members, April 18, 1972.

Chapter 8: A Caucus Convenes

83 For more information about Robert Drinan, see January 28, 2007, article in *The Boston Globe* by Mark Feeney, "Rev. Drinan, first priest elected as voting member of Congress, dies," http://archive.boston.com/news/globe/obituaries/articles/2007/01/28/rev_drinan_first_priest_elected_as_voting_member_of_congress_dies/.

84 Tip O'Neill, telephone calls to Democratic colleagues, April 18, 1972.

85 Tip O'Neill, Carl Albert, and Hale Boggs, conversation in the speaker's office during the caucus, April 19, 1972.

86 This is how the game of politics is played. The Nixon Administration had a highly effective lobbying organization, which worked on the dissident Southern conservative Democrats to muster support for Nixon policies. Whenever necessary, federal projects were given to the district of the Congress member who supported the Administration position on a specific piece of legislation.

87 Tip O'Neill, remarks made at Democratic Caucus, April 19, 1972.

88 Ibid.

89 Hale Boggs was very fond of the Whip and frequently congratulated O'Neill on a job well done. O'Neill and Boggs worked extremely well together and had become good friends as well as professional colleagues since Boggs had appointed O'Neill majority whip in 1971.

90 Tip O'Neill, remarks made at the Democratic caucus, April 19, 1972.

Chapter 9: Surprise, Surprise! Parliamentary Maneuvering

91 Ed Edmondson, resolution offered at the Democratic Caucus, *Journal of Proceedings of Democratic Caucus*, April 19, 1972.

92 Tip O'Neill, comment to Ed Edmondson in House chamber during the Democratic caucus, April 19, 1972.

93 O'Neill had lined up speakers who were regionally and ethnically diversified party regulars with excellent antiwar credentials: Sparky Matsunaga was O'Neill's colleague on the Rules Committee; John Brademas was a liberal Rhodes Scholar, Assistant Majority Whip, and ranking member of the Education and Labor Committee; Jack Flynt was a leading antiwar Southerner and member of the zone whip organization; Eddie Boland was O'Neill's roommate in Washington and chairman of the House Appropriations Subcommittee on HUD and Independent Agencies.

94 *Journal of Caucus Proceedings*, April 19, 1972.

95 Robert Drinan, remarks to the press, quoted by *The Washington Post*, April 20, 1972.

96 The closeness of O'Neill and Edmondson's professional friendship and their esteem for one another cannot be underestimated.

97 Leadership letter to committee chairmen, April 19, 1972.

98 Tip O'Neill, Carl Albert, and Hale Boggs, conversation in the speaker's office, April 19, 1972.

99 Tip O'Neill, letter to Democratic members, April 19, 1972.

100 Sam Gibbons, amendment to O'Neill substitute offered at Democratic Caucus, *Journal of Caucus Proceedings*, April 20, 1972.

101 Tip O'Neill, telephone call to Olin Teague, April 19, 1972.

102 This parliamentary maneuver—to challenge the Chairman by calling for a caucus vote—was worked out Wednesday afternoon among O'Neill, the legislative assistant, and Dave and Fred of Common Cause.

103 A congressional member may vote "yea" or "nay" or "present." By voting "present," the member is not officially taking a stand one way or the other.

104 *Journal of Caucus Proceedings*, April 20, 1972.

105 Ibid.

106 Robert Drinan, remarks to the press, April 20, 1972.

107 Tip O'Neill, remarks to the press, April 20, 1972.

108 Thomas Morgan, remarks to the press, April 20, 1972.

109 See chapter 4 for a detailed breakdown of voting on Senate amendments.

Chapter 10: Will the House Committee Accept Its Independent Role in Foreign Policy?

110 Standing House committees are permanent committees, for which jurisdiction is determined by the House Rules.

111 U.S. House of Representatives Committee on Foreign Affairs, https://foreignaffairs.house.gov; National Archives, "Records of the Foreign Affairs Committee," https://www.archives.gov/legislative/guide/house/chapter-10.html.

112 United States Senate Committee on Foreign Relations, "Committee History & Rules," https://www.foreign.senate.gov/about/history/.

113 Article II, section 2, of the U.S. Constitution; United States Senate, "Advice and Consent of the Senate," https://www.senate.gov/artandhistory/history/common/generic/Origins_AdviceConsent.htm.

114 U.S. Senate Committee on Foreign Relations, https://www.foreign.senate.gov/about/history/.

115 U.S. House Committee on Foreign Affairs, https://foreignaffairs.house.gov; National Archives, https://www.archives.gov/legislative/guide/house/chapter-10.html.

116 Clement Zablocki (Wisconsin), member of the House Foreign Affairs Committee, interview with the author, November 30, 1972.

117 Thomas Morgan, "Senate, House Committees Differ on Foreign Affairs," *Congressional Quarterly Weekly Report 28*, November 20, 1970, 2825.

118 Thomas Morgan (Pennsylvania), interview with the author, November 25, 1972.

119 Ibid.

120 Ibid.

121 Dante Fascell (Florida), interview with the author, November 15, 1972, and Zablocki interview, November 30, 1972.

122 See chapter 4 for a detailed breakdown of voting on Senate amendments.

123 These members shall remain anonymous.

Chapter 11: Thirty-Day Deadline

124 *War Powers Resolution: Hearings Before the Committee on Foreign Relations, United States Senate, Ninety-fifth Congress, on a Review of the Operation and Effectiveness of the War Power Resolution, July 13, 14, and 15, 1977* (Washington: U.S. Government Printing Office, 1977), 470.

125 Clement Zablocki, interview with the author, November 30, 1972.

126 Tip O'Neill and Clem Zablocki, conversation at whip coffee meeting, October 15, 1971.

127 Wayne Hays, overheard by the author.

128 These sources shall remain anonymous.

129 Marshall Frady provided an excellent description of Wayne Hays and the power he wields in the House in "Chairman Skinflint," published in *Playboy*, July 1973.

130 Dante Fascell, interview with the author, November 15, 1972.

131 Donald Fraser (Minnesota), interview with the author, November 15, 1972.

132 Lee Hamilton (Indiana), interview with the author, November 17, 1972.

133 Ibid.

134 Congressional Black Caucus, "About the CBC," https://cbc.house.gov/about/.

135 Conlin, Richard, "Impact and Implementation of the Caucus Indochina Resolution," April 24, 1972.

136 Ibid.

Chapter 12: A Committee Deliberates

137 Marcelo Ribeiro da Silva, "The Daring Plan to Mine Haiphong Harbor," https://www.historynet.com/the-daring-plan-to-mine-haiphong-harbor.htm.

138 Lee Hamilton, resolution offered at executive meeting of Democratic members of House Foreign Affairs Committee, May 10, 1972.

139 Clem Zablocki, resolution offered at executive meeting of Democratic members of House Foreign Affairs Committee, May 10, 1972.

140 Supported by North Vietnam, the Viet Cong were communist guerrilla forces that fought the South Vietnamese and U.S. forces in the Vietnam War.

141 John Buchanan, resolution offered at executive meeting of members of House Foreign Affairs Committee, June 13, 1972.

142 Committee vote on Buchanan resolution, June 13, 1972.

143 The two Republicans shall remain anonymous.

144 Dante Fascell, interview with the author, November 15, 1972.

145 John Buchanan, remarks to the press, quoted by *The Washington Post*, June 14, 1972.

146 Clem Zablocki, remarks to the press, quoted by *The Washington Post*, June 14, 1972.

147 Lee Hamilton, remarks to the press, quoted by *The Washington Post*, June 14, 1972.

148 Thomas Morgan, remarks to the press, quoted by *The Washington Post*, June 14, 1972.

149 Tip O'Neill, comment to the author.

150 Tip O'Neill, remarks to the press, quoted by *The Washington Post*, June 14, 1972.

151 Marion Czarnecki, Chief of Staff, House Foreign Affairs Committee, interview with the author, June 15, 1972.

152 Dante Fascell, interview with the author, November 5, 1972.

153 John W. Finney, "Foreign-Aid Bill Killed in Senate after Passage of End-War Amendment," *The New York Times*, July 25, 1972.

154 *Congressional Record*, Volume 157, Number 107, https://www.govinfo.gov/content/pkg/CREC-2011-07-18/html/CREC-2011-07-18-pt1-PgH5133-3.htm.

Chapter 13: A Tale of Two Dates: Section 13 and the Whalen Amendment

155 Rules Committee action on Foreign Assistance Act of 1972.

156 H.R. 16029, Foreign Assistance Act of 1972, Section 13.

157 Ibid.

158 *House Report 92-1273*, Foreign Assistance Act, "Additional Views of Honorable Lee Hamilton and Honorable Charles W. Whalen, Jr.," 29.

159 Ibid, 30.

160 Ibid, "Additional Views of Hon. Clement Zablocki, Hon. Wayne Hays, Hon. William Maillaird, Hon. John Buchanan, etc.," 22–23.

161 Ibid, 23.

162 Ibid, "Additional Views of Hon. Paul Findley," 33.

163 Ibid, "Additional Views of Hon. Guy Vander Jagt," 35.

164 Tip O'Neill, letter to Democratic members re. Morgan-Hamilton amendment, August 7, 1972.

165 John Gardner, quoted by *The Washington Post*, August 9, 1972.

166 Tip O'Neill, interview with the author, August 7, 1972.
167 Richard Nixon, quoted by *The Washington Post*, August 9, 1972.

Chapter 14: The House Casts a Vote: The Tragic Flaw of Committee Indecision

168 *Congressional Record*, August 10, 1972, H-7458.
169 Ibid, H-7469.
170 Ibid, H-7471.
171 Ibid, H-7477.
172 Ibid, H-7481.
173 Ibid, H-7481ff.
174 In a political context, optics is the way an action or event is perceived by the public.
175 *Congressional Record*, August 10, 1972, H-7481–82.
176 Ibid, H-7483.
177 Ibid, H-7485.
178 Ibid, H-7488.
179 Ibid, H-7485.
180 The representative shall remain anonymous; comment made to the author on the House floor, August 10, 1972.
181 Morgan and members of the House Foreign Affairs Committee later remarked.
182 This was O'Neill's analysis after he and the legislative assistant (this author) discussed the vote on both the Whalen and Bolling amendments.
183 Tip O'Neill, comment on the House floor after the vote on the Bolling amendment, August 10, 1972.

Chapter 15: The End of the War and the Beginning of a New House

184 History, Art, & Archives: United States House of Representatives, "BOGGS, Thomas Hale, Sr.," https://history.house.gov/People/Detail/9547.

185 Bruno Cooke, "What is a 'Saigon moment'? Meaning and history explored," *The Focus*, August 2021, https://www.thefocus.news/culture/saigon-moment-meaning/.

186 Office of the Historian, "U.S. Involvement in the Vietnam War: The Tet Offensive, 1968," https://history.state.gov/milestones/1961-1968/tet.

187 Richard L. Madden, "Sweeping Cutoff of Funds for War is Voted in Senate," *The New York Times*, June 15, 1973; *The Oxford Companion to American Military History*, "Case-Church Amendment," https://www.encyclopedia.com/history/encyclopedias-almanacs-transcripts-and-maps/case-church-amendment.

188 History.com editors, "Vietnam War Timeline," February 26, 2020, https://www.history.com/topics/vietnam-war/vietnam-war-timeline.

189 H.J.Res. 542, the War Powers Act, was adopted as Public Law 93-148 on November 7, 1973.

190 H.J.Res. 542, Public Law 93-148.

191 Tip O'Neill, from conversation with the legislative assistant re. Zablocki's request.

192 October 20, 1973: Nixon fired the U.S. solicitor general, Special Prosecutor Archibald Cox, and accepted resignations for Attorney General Elliot Richardson and Deputy Attorney General William Ruckelshaus, who refused to fire Cox despite Nixon's order.

193 Tip O'Neill, comments made to the author.

194 The Presentment Clause requires any bills that pass both the House and the Senate to be presented to the President for signature or veto of whole bill.

195 H.R. 1457 (117th Congress).

196 Karoun Demirjian, "Bipartisan bill aims to assert Congress's power over arms sales, emergencies and military operations," *The Washington Post*, July 20, 2021.

197 Arthur M. Schlesinger Jr., *The Imperial Presidency* (Boston: Houghton Mifflin, 1973).

198 History, Art, & Archives: United States House of Representatives, "Congressional Budget and Impoundment Control Act of 1974," https://history.house.gov/Historical-Highlights/1951-2000/Congressional-Budget-and-Impoundment-Control-Act-of-1974/.

199 John A. Lawrence, "How the 'Watergate Babies' Broke American Politics," *Politico Magazine*, May 26, 2018.

200 Rutgers Eagleton Institute of Politics, Center for American Women and Politics, "History of Women in the U.S. Congress," https://cawp.rutgers.edu/history-women-us-congress.

201 Connecticut Women's Hall of Fame, "Ella Tambussi Grasso," https://www.cwhf.org/inductees/ella-tambussi-grasso.

202 Tip O'Neill to Peter Rodino, as witnessed by the author.

203 *A History of the Committee on the Judiciary 1813–2006*, 120, https://www.govinfo.gov/content/pkg/GPO-CDOC-109hdoc153/pdf/GPO-CDOC-109hdoc153-3-1.pdf.

204 History staff, "The Watergate Scandal: A Timeline," August 3, 2021, https://www.history.com/topics/watergate-scandal-timeline-nixon.

205 Author's conversations with Pete Rodino and Leo Diehl.

206 History staff, "The Watergate Scandal: A Timeline," August 3, 2021, https://www.history.com/topics/watergate-scandal-timeline-nixon.

Chapter 16: A New Era: The House Democratized

207 EveryCRSReport.com, October 20, 2003, https://www.everycrsreport.com/reports/RL31835.html.

208 Rutgers Eagleton Institute, CAWP, "Women in Congress: Leadership Roles and Committee Chairs," https://cawp.rutgers.edu/women-congress-leadership-committees; History, Art, & Archives: United States House of Representatives, "Women in Congress: Historical Data," https://history.house.gov/Exhibitions-and-Publications/WIC/Historical-Data/Historical-Data---Nav/.

209 History, Art, & Archives: United States House of Representatives, "The House and Television," https://history.house.gov/Exhibitions-and-Publications/Electronic-Technology/Television/.

210 Ibid.

211 University of Virginia, Miller Center, "Barbara Jordan remarks on impeachment during Watergate," https://millercenter.org/the-presidency/impeachment/my-faith-constitution-whole-it-complete-it-total.

212 History, Art, & Archives: United States House of Representatives, "Stories from the People's House: Go All the Way," May 24, 2017, https://history.house.gov/Blog/2017/May/5-24-Obey-Commission/.

213 Encyclopedia Britannica editors, "Exodus," *Encyclopedia Britannica*, July 26, 2021, https://www.britannica.com/event/Exodus-Old-Testament.

214 Jimmy Carter to Tip O'Neill, as told to the author.

Chapter 17: The House's Rightful Role Restored?

215 History, Art, & Archives: United States House of Representatives, "92nd Congress (1971–1973)," https://history.house.gov/Congressional-Overview/Profiles/92nd/.

Epilogue

216 "Text of Havel's Speech to Congress," *The Washington Post*, https://www.washingtonpost.com/archive/politics/1990/02/22/text-of-havels-speech-to-congress/df98e177-778e-4c26-bd96-980089c4fcb2/.

217 Michelle Obama, *Becoming* (New York: Crown, 2018): "When you've worked hard, and done well, and walked through that doorway of opportunity, you do not slam it shut behind you. You reach back and you give other folks the same chances that helped you succeed."

218 Mike Mansfield, quoted by Adam Nossiter in *The New York Times*, "America's Afghan War: A Defeat Foretold?" August 21, 2021.

219 Elliot Ackerman, "The Botched Afghanistan Withdrawal Exposes a Dangerous Faultline in Our Democracy," *TIME*, August 31, 2021.

220 Adam Andrzejewski, "Staggering Costs—U.S. Military Equipment Left Behind in Afghanistan," *Forbes*, August 23, 2021.

221 Adam Nossiter, "America's Afghan War," *The New York Times*, August 21, 2021.

222 Ibid.

Author BIO

The first woman Majority Leader of the Massachusetts Senate, Linda managed and led the state Senate on public policy issues. As Senate Chairwoman of the Insurance Committee, she was responsible for all major health insurance legislation enacted in the Commonwealth and created a legislative Science and Technology Committee to pioneer nationally recognized laws on genetic testing and life science. Recognized and honored as "Majority Leader Emerita" for her passion, hard work, energy, and acute negotiation skills, Linda advocated empowerment, diversity, dialogue, teamwork, and shared vision.

Prior to serving in the Massachusetts Senate, Linda was Assistant Counsel to the late U.S. House of Representatives Speaker Thomas P. "Tip" O'Neill Jr. Among the first women staff professionals to merit standing U.S. House floor privileges in all three majority leadership offices, she also held positions of chief legislative assistant and speechwriter, House floor member assistant, and domestic and foreign policy advisor. She was honored by the Armenian community for her staff role in creating April 24 as a national commemoration of the Armenian genocide.

Currently, Linda teaches public policy and non-profit and business law courses at Suffolk University. As a Senior Fellow in the Moakley Center for Public Management, she designs unique program opportunities, connecting business students with government leaders: for example, a Moakley Fellows Graduate Internship Program in Washington, D.C., and a Moakley Breakfast Forum Series to engage Greater Boston communities on current public policy issues at the federal, state, and local levels.

Linda presents at forums, conferences, panels, and summits on gender leadership in the political arena. She contributes to the Weissman Center for Leadership and the Liberal Arts at Mount Holyoke College, enhancing its course offerings on leadership for women. As an advisor and consultant to American International College, she enriched its MPA program and developed its MSNPM course of study. Recently, she served on Greenfield Community College's Board of Trustees.

Her published material on political leadership include "Lead and Win: 78 keys and strategies"; "Applied Leadership," a book chapter; "Gender Pay Equality: Effectiveness of Federal Statutes and Recent U.S. Supreme Court Decisions," *Public Policy Forum Journal,* 2010. She co-authored the following legal and scholarly articles: "Health-care Nonprofits: Enhancing Governance and Public Trust," *Journal of Business and Society Review,* 2011; "Evolving Corporate Governance Standards for Health Care Nonprofits: Is Board Compensation a

Breach of Fiduciary Duty?" *Brooklyn Journal of Corporate Financial Commercial Law,* 2013; "Enhancing Business Ethics and Governance Curriculum: Teaching Nonprofit Organizational Governance," *Journal of Academy of Business Education,* 2014; "State Oversight of Nonprofit Governance: Confronting the Challenge of Mission Adherence within a Multi-Dimensional Standard," *Journal of Law and Commerce at the University of Pittsburgh School of Law,* 2014; "Social Enterprise: Reaffirming Public Purpose Governance Through Shared Value," *Michigan State University Journal of Business and Securities Law*, 2016.

A *cum laude* graduate of Mount Holyoke College, Linda earned a Master's Degree (M.A.) from the School of Public and International Affairs at George Washington University and a Doctor of Jurisprudence (J.D.) from George Mason University. In 2012, she was inducted into Suffolk University's chapter of Pi Alpha Alpha, the national honor society for public affairs and administration, for "Scholarship-Leadership-Excellence." Mount Holyoke College honored Linda that same year as one of its 175 alumnae "Women of Influence." The Suffolk University Student Government Association honored her with the 2018 Dean John Brennan Award for "Outstanding Instruction to Graduate Students."

In 2019, she participated in the U.S. House of Representatives Historian's Office Oral History Project commemorating the 100th anniversary of the first woman elected to Congress.

She and her husband, Andrew J. Scibelli, reside in Springfield, Massachusetts.

Made in the USA
Middletown, DE
07 April 2022